Job Crafting

Management on the Cutting Edge series

Abbie Lundberg, series editor

Published in cooperation with *MIT Sloan Management Review*

MITSloan
Management Review

Job Crafting

Benjamin Laker, Lebene Soga,
Yemisi Bolade-Ogunfodun, and Adeyinka Adewale

The MIT Press
Cambridge, Massachusetts
London, England

The MIT Press would like to thank the anonymous peer reviewers who provided comments on drafts of this book. The generous work of academic experts is essential for establishing the authority and quality of our publications. We acknowledge with gratitude the contributions of these otherwise uncredited readers.

This book was set in Stone Serif and Stone Sans by Westchester Publishing Services. Printed and bound in the United States of America.

Library of Congress Cataloging-in-Publication Data

Names: Laker, Ben (Benjamin), author.
Title: Job crafting / Benjamin Laker, Lebene Soga, Yemisi Bolade-Ogunfodun, and Adeyinka Adewale.
Description: Cambridge, Massachusetts : The MIT Press, [2024] |
  Series: Management on the cutting edge series | Includes bibliographical references and index.
Identifiers: LCCN 2023028856 (print) | LCCN 2023028857 (ebook) |
  ISBN 9780262048880 (hardcover) | ISBN 9780262378031 (epub) |
  ISBN 9780262378024 (pdf)
Subjects: LCSH: Quality of work life. | Job satisfaction. | Flexible work arrangements. | Personnel management. | Organizational effectiveness.
Classification: LCC HD6955 .L25 2024 (print) | LCC HD6955 (ebook) |
  DDC 658.3/14—dc23/eng/20230720
LC record available at https://lccn.loc.gov/2023028856
LC ebook record available at https://lccn.loc.gov/2023028857

10 9 8 7 6 5 4 3 2 1

Contents

Series Foreword

The world does not lack for management ideas. Thousands of researchers, practitioners, and other experts produce tens of thousands of articles, books, papers, posts, and podcasts each year. But only a scant few promise to truly move the needle on practice, and fewer still dare to reach into the future of what management will become. It is this rare breed of idea—meaningful to practice, grounded in evidence, and *built for the future*—that we seek to present in this series.

Abbie Lundberg
Editor in chief
MIT Sloan Management Review

Preface: Why This Book?

We set out to write this book in response to some of the seismic shifts in the world of work that require managers and leaders of organizations, as well as the teams they lead, to act decisively. At the core of these shifts are changes to the way we work and the impact these changes have on our engagement with work and our understanding of meaningful work.

During the pandemic and in the year after most containment measures were lifted, the employee experience came to the fore. Before COVID-19, Gallup reported, 13 percent of employees felt actively disengaged at work, and only around 35 percent of employees reported feeling actively engaged.[1] That figure has not changed much since then. As more people take on side gigs, the risk of employee disengagement increases because workers now have another demand on their time and effort. For example, suppose the salaried team leader is overly critical or given to micromanagement. In that case, the employees who report to the team leader can tune out and channel their skills and attention into their side hustle, where they are the boss. As the post-COVID workplace situation gradually settles into a new normalcy, employers might be hoping for a return to business as usual, but, perhaps unknown to them, they now have competitors, people or agencies who hire their employees for freelance jobs. Today the danger is less that employees will simply quit than that they will continue in their jobs, but disengaged in mind and spirit. It's a challenging situation that requires leaders to step up in new ways if they want their best employees to remain engaged at work.

Seventy-six percent of white-collar workers are considering quitting or changing their jobs as burnout, a poor corporate culture, and long hours continue to bite. The figures come from a nationwide, census-wide survey commissioned by Juno, a workplace well-being marketplace in 2022.[2] The survey polled one thousand white-collar workers, ranging from entry-level grads through senior managers, for their views on workplace morale, burnout, toxicity, and mental health in the modern work environment. The survey findings showed that white-collar workers were suffering from low morale, with the situation spiraling as a result of current labor shortages in the economy. And as shortages bite, prospective recruits are indicating that pastoral matters such as work-life balance, company culture, and mental health at work are more important than salary (58 percent favored pastoral issues, 23 percent favored pay).[3]

An astonishing 57 percent of all employees are currently experiencing low morale in the workplace, a figure that rises to 62 percent for those aged forty-five to fifty-four years old. A further 40 percent of employees say their firm has to operate at a reduced capacity because of shortages, and 15 percent are seeing sales fall as they struggle to meet customer demand because of short staffing.[4] For several companies, this is creating a vicious circle whereby staff shortages worsen employee morale, which contributes to employee turnover, which exacerbates the economic impact of shortages on the firm's performance. A staggering 70 percent of workers would leave their current role if they had another job to go to, with this figure rising to 80 percent among eighteen- to twenty-four-year-olds.

There are a number of reasons for this situation, first and foremost being the pandemic. Research shows that 71 percent of employees saw an increase in workload starting from the beginning of the pandemic, with 67 percent of those saying the increase was unmanageable.[5] This had a knock-on effect on mental health, with 56 percent of employees reporting they felt anxious or depressed since the pandemic began. Throughout the UK economy, the situation amplified issues around burnout, workplace toxicity, and stress. Research showed that in 2022,

21 percent of employees in white-collar jobs became indifferent toward the company they worked for, 19 percent reported their mental and physical health had suffered, and 18 percent believed they had been working in a toxic environment.[6]

A war for talent is taking place on two fronts—keeping employees happy and hiring new ones. The "Great Resignation" of 2021 through early 2023 reached an all-time high at the end of June 2022, creating 10.1 million job openings.[7] Termination rates remained the same, but the number of people quitting their jobs increased. The reasons for the job vacancies were manifold but boiled down to a basic dynamic: an increase in the number of job openings and a decrease in the number of people looking for work. In other words, there were more opportunities for workers to find new jobs and fewer people competing for those jobs. Under these market pressures, employers competing for talent had to offer higher wages and better benefits. The situation was exacerbated by growing firm worry over reputational costs as boycotts and social media call-outs targeting poor firm experiences became more common. A bad reputation can make it hard to attract top talent, and even harder to keep the talent you have. As such, many companies began trying to improve their workplace culture, with mixed success. The pandemic also put a spotlight on the importance of work-life balance, with many people working from home. Companies started to see the benefits of flexible working arrangements, and employees began to prioritize flexible arrangements in their job searches. In one poll, 54 percent of workers said they would leave their current job if it didn't offer flexible working arrangements.[8] To sum up, the economy began facing a war for talent on two fronts, with companies needing to attract new employees while retaining the ones they already had. And in both cases, culture is key.

Already struggling to fill open positions, companies today are making extra efforts to try to keep more employees from quitting. They're raising pay, adding more bonuses, paying for college, increasing vacation days, and hiring thank you robots. That's right: instead of taking humans' jobs, robots are now trying to keep humans employed by writing them thank you notes. The thinking is that if the work environment is made more fun, employees will be less likely to want to leave. But these methods are only Band-Aids that fail to address a much deeper problem. As the job market begins to recover, are employers prepared for it? More than half the global workforce (54 percent) say they are prepared to leave a job lacking flexibility and remote working options. This is according to research by Instant Offices, global workspace specialists, which revealed that nine out of ten office workers want more flexibility in where and when they do their job—and more than half of them are willing to leave if they don't get it.[9] Another survey by EY (Ernst & Young Pvt.) revealed that 54 percent of workers worldwide would consider leaving their current job after the pandemic if their employees didn't offer more flexibility.[10] That suggests that the pandemic increased the demand for flexible working arrangements and that employees are now more likely to leave a job that doesn't offer them. More crucial, however, is the understated yet obvious need for employees to be actively engaged in their own job design, which makes their overall experience more fulfilling.

Recently released results of a benchmark report in June 2021 by SAPinsider, the largest and fastest-growing SAP professionals community worldwide, titled *The State of Human Experience in the Workplace*, based on the responses of 111 members of its global community, sought to understand important factors shaping employee experiences in the workplace and to uncover strategies that might mitigate negative experiences.[11] The research found that the traditional nine-to-five workday is no longer the norm, with 37 percent of employees working remotely full-time and a further 21 percent working remotely some of the time. Interestingly, the growing demand for flexibility at work is reflected in the high number of jobs with remote work offered now becoming available. For example, in July 2021 alone, Glassdoor posted over 80,000 jobs advertised as "remote" and 490,000 advertised as "flexible." Meanwhile, only one in ten employers expected their employees to revert to prepandemic working arrangements, including a full return to the office. Most of these are companies operating in the services sector. There are currently a record one million job vacancies open in the UK. (A common assumption is that the vacancies are mostly in manual and blue- or pink-collar work, such as leisure, retail, and construction.) In a May 2021 study conducted by HiBob, only 14 percent of employees indicated they wanted to return to the office full-time, with more than a third stating they would quit if required to return to the office five days a week.[12] Flexibility is the future of work. HR teams must put together plans that align with this understanding. Better work-life balance is becoming increasingly key in addition to good compensation not only to attracting new talent but also to retaining current employees. To foster high levels of happiness, productivity, and satisfaction among your workforce, incorporating hybrid work scheduling is a must.

One might expect salary demands to be the most prominent factor in why a job candidate may choose one role over another. However, Juno's data suggest that job candidates are much more concerned about their wellness at work, the corporate culture, and work-life balance than they are about financial gain.[13] Around 23 percent of respondents in Juno's 2022 survey said that salary demands were the primary reason a potential candidate chose a different job offer. In addition, a combined 58 percent of respondents said that a better work-life balance or better workplace culture at the rival company, improved benefits (childcare, health care), and improved access to wellness tools were the factors behind a prospective employee choosing an alternative role and employer. With many employees forced to move to partial or fully remote working arrangements and with deskless workers evaluating their options with alternative companies and roles, employers are seeking new ways to engage existing and potential recruits.

The State of Human Experience in the Workplace 2022 also provides insight into where organizations currently are on their employee experience management journey.[14] With respect to challenges that organizations had faced over the previous few years, the study found that retaining top talent (cited by 26 percent of respondents) and maintaining employee engagement (cited by 23 percent) were two of the top three challenges. The study further provides important insights into where organizations are currently with their employee experience management strategies, with the majority of respondents indicating that the pandemic was the largest driver of change, forcing them to reconsider how to maintain or improve employee engagement at work. With respect to employee experience drivers, many companies said that optimizing access to employee and work data was their lead action (a response selected by 61 percent of respondents) and investing in technology to improve worker productivity was a tactic utilized by 59 percent. In comparison, 54 percent of respondents said creating spaces and processes to increase collaboration between employees and teams was a main focus.

Additionally, nearly 50 percent of respondents were adding or improving employee feedback or surveys to capture their employees' sentiment so that the organizations could better react in the moment to increase employee satisfaction. However, as Terence Mauri, founder of Hack Future Lab and an entrepreneur mentor in residence at MIT, has said in an interview with one of the authors:

> To paraphrase Einstein, you can't use an old map to navigate a new world. Organizations must not miss out on the biggest reframing moment of their lifetimes. A major inflection point is the New Human Equation, which simply means humans want Meaning Maximization, not just Profit Maximization: more purpose, more opportunity, and more freedom to decide their own career pathways. Old ways of working, leading, and learning are being upended with paradigm shifts from career ladders to career climbing walls, fixed mindset to a growth mindset, and a "do one thing workforce" to a "do anything workforce." The future will be won by those who scale Return on Intelligence, not just return on investment. The challenges associated with mending old ways of work, including opportunities for staff to access workforce flexibility to manage their work and life domains effectively, are riddled with policy and business case imperatives.[15]

These findings raise questions of what meaningful work and meaningfulness at work are to employees; perhaps more important, they challenge organizations to find new ways to engage and connect with their employees wherever the latter may be. These past few years have shown us that businesses that can pivot and be flexible and attentive to their employees' changing needs will gain a competitive edge and the opportunity to thrive. Investing in business operations that have a direct positive impact on employees' day-to-day work experience also has an impact on customers' satisfaction as organizations strive for greater customer and employee retention. This book offers a blueprint for how organizations can become more proactive and intentional in how they sustain and improve the engagement of their employees through job crafting.

Job crafting is presented in this book as a vital tool for helping employees connect with their purpose and motivation; hence we move it from "another HR practice" to a cultural phenomenon that should be at the center of how organizations are designed, function, and thrive. We expect the book to spark debates and conversations, but also to help leaders, managers, and organizations think through their practices with a view to making necessary changes that benefit the most vital resource of the organization—the people at its center.

Consequently, our book offers practical guidance to line managers and executives from a perspective that is empowering and inclusive for their employees. Readers should walk away not only understanding the model discussed herein but also with acquired knowledge regarding how it can be implemented to empower the workers they manage to transform the jobs they have into the jobs they want. It is grounded in empirical evidence, primarily for executives, and specifically for those who manage others. We offer them applicable knowledge and step-by-step guidance regarding how managers can put in place the systems, structures, and processes needed workers to undertake job crafting. The narrative combines description with analysis to support secondary sources such as empirical propositions adduced from interviews conducted in a previous study by one of the authors with business leaders and their workers around the world (67.1 percent from North America and 32.9 percent from the UK and Australia) in Fortune 200 firms, including Apple, American Express, Cisco, Dow, JPMorgan Chase, and Microsoft.[16] As a result, the book is expected to appeal primarily to business executives who wish to transform their organizations by driving structural change, developing employee training programs using evidence-based techniques, or creating an innovative organizational culture. Insights from the book should also be useful in executive education programs, including MBA programs, because of their practical application.

The eight chapters of the book collectively address why job crafting is important in the modern firm, the main types of job crafting (cognitive, relational, and task crafting), individual and organizational readiness for job crafting, and permission to craft. The later chapters of the book explore how organizations can create safe spaces for job crafting, develop tools for job crafting, and build capacity to job craft, with the concluding chapter summarizing the key thoughts from the preceding chapters. We hope this book contributes to your journey toward building stronger, more inclusive, and more rewarding organizations where everyone feels valued, connected, and fully engaged.

1 Why Job Crafting?

There is something artistic about the word "craft." To craft comes from the Anglo-Saxon word *cræft*, which denotes "strength, power, might." It implicitly suggests an active, purposeful shaping that alters the form of an object. It also speaks to the skills of the crafter and implies suitable conditions exist for undertaking the activity. An intrinsic sense of worth and satisfaction experienced as a result of fully engaging in the act of immense interest, that is, the expression of creative freedom, is at the root of the meaningfulness such an artistic endeavor provides. Hence, engaging in crafting implies the space to create, high levels of engagement, and ultimately the enjoyment of meaningful work.

To remain true to the root meaning of the word, then, job crafting becomes necessary in conditions that are potentially unfavorable, requiring the individual to deploy strength, power, and might in order to survive or flourish in that work environment. No "cræfting" would be warranted in a fully functioning, machine-like organization that had all things working to plan. It would be a perfect system. Unsurprisingly, this is also the weakness of systems theory approaches to organizations, in which a system is commonly viewed as a set of subsystems organized for a common purpose or goal. In contrast, the modern organization today is viewed as a political entity, which shifts the focus to the different actors, groups, tribes, functional units, departments, committees, teams, hierarchies, and so forth that pursue their own interests as much as those of the organization.

However, crafting may not be the default setting with jobs in organizations, especially those that require job descriptions to be strictly followed, with minimal room for employees to innovate. At this moment in history, during which several macro variables affect how organizations design work that affects how employees see themselves in their jobs, it is vital to explore how organizations can ensure their employees enjoy meaningful work. Doing so becomes even more urgent if employees—a firm's actual human resource—are valued as the most precious assets of the organization. In this chapter we explore the why, what, and how of job crafting, with specific attention to how the current state of societies, organizations, and individuals creates the need for job crafting.

Why Job Crafting?

Students of workplace phenomena have conceptualized job crafting in similar ways. In the main, however, it is seen as a mechanism to achieve a balance between work elements that incite pleasure and those elements that destroy joy by taking into account three dimensions of workers' roles: what workers do, why they do it, and with whom they work. The concept of job crafting is not a new one. However, recent interest addresses how it has been beneficial in work contexts. As a result, it has become popular with HR practitioners, organization leaders, and employees themselves.

Leadership theorist David Pendleton and his co-authors point out that the classic job design model is employer-centered, with employees relegated to the passive margins. This perspective can be understood when job creation is viewed historically, against the backdrop of organizational structure intended to support a post–World War I society and aimed at industrial production efficiency. Traditional bureaucratic and role-driven organizational structures often retain such classic approaches to job design. If a job is to be redesigned, therefore, it would have to be adapted to organizational needs to facilitate productivity. Though efficiency has a place in job design, the dynamism in the contemporary workplace and the fast pace of change create challenging contexts for organizations. Additionally, there has been a shift in some sectors to postbureaucratic forms of organization characterized by more personalized approaches to job creation and design. As well, research suggests that traditional workplace jobs that have existed for decades are being replaced by "jobs of the future," requiring new roles such as digital content creator, social media influencer, IT administrator, and the like.

Given the changes in the workplace in both customer and employee needs, managers find it incumbent to make adjustments so that desired organizational outcomes can be achieved. An increasingly globalized world has created interdependencies across industries and markets such that economic changes in one sector or one part of the world have ripple effects on others. As a result, businesses and leaders operate and make decisions in unpredictable and volatile environments. While advances in leadership research have begun to shift the focus to more employee-centered approaches to leadership, research shows that there is still a long way to go to achieve true employee engagement. Alongside these changes, employee needs have begun to take center stage in the workplace. A notable event that further contributed to the salience of changing employee needs is the global COVID-19 pandemic, which had a significant and, in some cases, life-changing impact on employees. Empirical evidence indicates that many employees lost their jobs, while others moved to primarily home-based work. The protracted period of socially distanced work had some unintended consequences, such as providing space for employees to reflect on their priorities, their values, and how work was contributing to their achieving a meaningful life. Employees became more willing to move away from certain types of roles that crowded out what they considered important, such as time with family, work flexibility, empowerment, autonomy, recognition, and opportunities for advancement. These multidimensional changes have opened the door for interrogating meaning in work, separate from formal role requirements. In this dynamic context, the focus on work quality and meaning presents opportunities for managerial job crafting.

This is particularly beneficial for managers who are faced with employees choosing to take the plunge and leave work in which they are unable to find meaning, or employees who choose to continue in such employment but who might approach their roles and relationships differently. These changes in employee behavior may necessitate that managers adopt strategies to craft their own roles in ways that allow them to respond to emerging challenges in the workplace. Not only do managers benefit from finding meaning in their work, they must also create conditions for an engaged workforce to emerge. In an ideal situation, employeeship, in which traditional hierarchical relationships are set aside with the aim of "creat[ing] partnerships between managers and employees . . . and mutual responsibility for their work," is a manager's dream. Employeeship is a laudable goal; however, the mechanisms by which that goal is pursued often fail to take into account those factors that are responsible for driving employee engagement. Such factors are important components of managerial decision-making. In a highly competitive and volatile working world, managers must plan and make decisions that have an impact on employees' expressed and unexpressed desires and expectations. What drives job crafting, therefore, is the search for meaning in work in relation to what is done, with whom, and why, in a way that organizational outcomes are still achieved. As a modern form of job design, job crafting exemplifies empowerment directed toward designing meaningful engagement with the workplace. Insofar as job crafting bestows on the individual an element of control, it offers an attractive space for job enrichment for managers despite novel changes in the workplace, in work relationships, and in the self. This is because it allows the fusing of key aspects of an individual's identity and interests with the work the individual does. We explore what job crafting is and its main types in the next section and next chapter, respectively.

What Is Job Crafting?

Job crafting is the proactive and intentional altering of one's job demands and resources to better fit one's own goals, strengths, and weaknesses. It was first introduced by Timothy D. Wilson and Mihaly

Csikszentmihalyi in their paper titled "Job Crafting: The Core of Active Job Creation" as a way to increase workers' control over their daily lives and improve workplace engagement.[1] A good starting point for thinking about it is to think about how to sustain employee engagement in a topsy-turvy postpandemic world where employee needs and demands are constantly evolving.

Engagement has been defined in several ways, but a fundamental underlying principle is that something about the self is consciously brought into the work environment to pursue specified goals. One definition of employee engagement considers it a process whereby "people employ and express themselves physically, cognitively, emotionally, and mentally during role performances."[2] Hence it does not involve the superficial analysis of staff engagement surveys conducted annually or twice a year by the HR team, and indeed, it goes beyond employees complying with organizational policies and norms. Rather, employee engagement is concerned with employees' feeling of connection to the organization and to one another despite changes in working practices, such as the shift to remote work, now increasingly common. It also concerns helping employees understand how their potentially changing roles and contributions deliver value to the business, and supporting employees through their mental, physical, and financial challenges. From this perspective, having employees engaged in meaningful work is critical to realizing organizational objectives. A focus on employee engagement, therefore, sets aside the "simply getting the job done" mindset in favor of the "giving more by bringing one's whole self to work" perspective.

Job crafting can take different forms, but the end goal is always to make the job more satisfying and engaging for the employee. This may entail the employee taking on new responsibilities or learning new skills, or the manager and employee jointly changing the way work is approached. For example, office workers who feel undervalued and unengaged in their current position might respond well, where the laws permit, to taking on assignments and responsibilities outside their job description if those assignments offer challenge and increase the workers' value to the company. Or retail workers who feel they're treated like replaceable cogs in a machine might embrace opportunities for greater interaction with customers to create a more personal connection with them. No matter what form it takes, job crafting is always about making the job more satisfying and engaging for the employee.

Job crafting is not a new concept, but it has taken on new significance in recent years as the world of work has changed dramatically. Employees are no longer content to sit back and let their careers happen to them—they want to be proactive and take control of their own destinies in the workplace. As a result, job crafting has become an increasingly popular way for employees to try to make their jobs more fulfilling and meaningful. In this regard, some conditions and policies create favorable environments for bringing one's whole self to work and have been noted to unleash employees' creativity.[3] As examples, employees may become involved in designing their own job, or a firm may commit to creating a safe psychosocial environment for everyone who works there. Organizational level factors such as these create the framework within which employees work. However, it is crucial to recognize that supplying these conditions and policies may not be enough to bring about engagement, as personal factors will make some employees more suited or more responsive to an organization than others (we discuss these factors later). Similarly, at the individual level, the underutilization or nonutilization of an employee's skills is directly linked to disengagement, and disengagement results in low productivity, which ultimately affects the business's bottom line.[4] According to Gallup's research, 70 percent of workers don't consider themselves engaged and want their jobs and current roles to be more satisfying, meaningful, and fulfilling. An estimated $500 million is lost annually in productivity as a result of disengagement.[5] Recent studies also conclude that employees are switching off because their skills aren't fully utilized, they are not challenged or stimulated, and they lack flexibility and autonomy.[6] Having unutilized or underutilized talent suggests that employees cannot genuinely account for their contributions to the organization, leading to a loss of meaning in work. Where employees feel their contributions are valuable, where they are free to make mistakes and be themselves while at work, they are more likely to be engaged.

For managers, then, determining how to improve employee engagement and satisfaction is a mission-critical priority. It is particularly salient when societal conditions alter working patterns. Such conditions might take the form of global disruptions to work as it is conventionally known, such as we have in a postpandemic world. Enforced social distancing requirements during the pandemic brought about significant shifts in working practices. Additionally, the negative economic consequences of slowed business growth created uncertainty regarding jobs, job redesign, and job security. Furthermore, while technology has kept some companies going, it has also widened gaps in work relationships, many of which are now conducted on such platforms as Microsoft Teams, Zoom, or WebEx. In other words, organizational, personal, and societal factors give rise to conditions that make it impossible for workers to understand their roles in the larger organization and define the boundaries of work. The discussion around work today has shifted to how we view work. As highlighted by Ann Francke, CEO of the Chartered Management Institute, at the CMI Women Conference 2023, "Work is no longer a place today; it is a task."[7] With this sea change in perspective, it's time to change how we approach work, by creating a process whereby workers can take proactive steps to redesign and personalize their roles. Job crafting is one approach being utilized to this end in a rapidly changing work context.

Job crafting is a proactive, often unsupervised, modern take on job design that empowers workers to transform their jobs into the jobs they want by becoming design agents instead of passive recipients of job titles, responsibilities, and roles. The premise is that workers can stay in the same position but derive more meaning from their jobs simply by changing aspects of what they do, how they interact with others, and how they think about their work. Essentially, crafting is a worker-driven practice that the modern workforce can use to make current roles into the jobs individual workers want and to build in flexibility from a position of purpose. Job crafting as discussed in this book has three dimensions: cognitive crafting, task crafting, and relational crafting. Each of these dimensions of crafting has benefits that transcend the benefits derived by the individual, for they have a positively impact on the organization as a whole.

The first dimension, cognitive crafting, relates to altering one's perception of the meaning of work. It is an essential step in job crafting as it provides an anchor for the other forms of job crafting. For example, it involves changing how employees mentally define the boundaries of jobs as a conscious intellectual undertaking (this relates to task crafting) and has a role to play in building relationships at work (relational crafting). Cognitive crafting is a challenging dimension of job crafting as employees are confronted with the daily routines of what they are first of all contracted to do, yet they must maintain a vision of their redefined or recrafted work. They must juxtapose their work contract with some sense of what they want their work to look like, taking into consideration the more significant organizational objectives and broader societal context.[8] Cognitive crafting requires employees to flex beyond their functional role to take on additional projects that play to their strengths and interests even as they keep their focus on organizational objectives. For example, a qualified accountant interested in marketing may want to get involved in a project with a communications or social media element. As a result, the crux of cognitive crafting is for the employee to cognitively allocate resources to the outputs assigned to his or her primary job function and be willing to take on additional projects that provide different rewards. Reimagining work in a postpandemic era where individuals work either entirely remotely or on hybrid teams means that we consider work as also beyond the brick-and-mortar boundaries the office space suggests. In other words, the organization is seen as a boundaryless entity whose work activities possess some form of fluidity so that employees are not creatively restricted as to what is possible in their role. Therefore, employees can be allowed to own their job freely and cognitively craft what they find satisfying about their job, even if that was not initially considered part of their responsibilities. This mental posture opens up a new way of thinking about what work means for employees. If employees find meaning in their job, they will give their best effort. Cognitive crafting allows employees to create and deliver value in their job, first to themselves and then to those they serve—in this case, the organization's clientele. We explore further in chapter 5 how cognitive crafting can be promoted by the organization.

The second dimension of job crafting, task crafting, relates to changing the job's task boundaries. Task crafting is about making changes to the task content, process, and outcome expectations of a job. It involves taking on new tasks or reengineering existing ones. For example, office workers may want to add more social interaction to their job by working closely with colleagues on a project or brainstorming over lunch instead of working independently at their desk all day. A salesperson may want to increase the level of customer service she provides by following up with customers after a purchase to ensure they are satisfied. Task crafting also involves taking on new tasks that were not part of the original job description but fall within the realm of possibilities for the employee. For example, an accountant may want to take on a marketing project or a human resources coordinator may want to help with event planning. By task crafting, employees can add more meaning to their work and make it more satisfying. Employees create a different position by choosing to do fewer, more, or different tasks than those prescribed in the formal job listing. This "different" job is a reconceptualization of the job and may not necessarily be another kind of job altogether. This reconceptualization readjusts the mindset, particularly in how the employee derives meaning and purpose from work. On the surface, nothing in the employee's contract visibly changes, but there are shifts in motivation and orientation that drive employee actions related to achieving organizational goals. This new mindset means that employees can now internalize the bigger purpose of the organization and align their work accordingly. It also means that they recognize the importance of their contribution to the bigger picture. For example, according to the story, when asked, "What do you do?," one janitor at NASA is said to have replied, "I'm helping put a man on the Moon."[9]

The janitor could also have replied, "I clean at NASA," without any reference to the purpose of the wider organization. However, in that example, the janitor would have considered the work not only as janitorial but also as putting men on the Moon. The implication is that a janitor may see a switch that he knows is always on, and ask why on a particular day it is off, although observing the switch may not be part of his contractual responsibilities. Asking this question might be what saves the technical activities of another department on that day. For another example, imagine a cleaner at a TV station who turns off the channel's servers switch to plug in the vacuum cleaner every morning. The company loses several million pounds in advertising revenue. Several experts try to solve this "technical" problem, and huge amounts of money are spent, only for someone to discover that the solution is a switch that is regularly turned off at specific times when it should be on. This employee saw his task as cleaning, nothing more. This narrow view of employees means that they fail to see the bigger picture and therefore are not alert to how their actions may or may not contribute to that bigger picture. In task crafting, employees are motivated and alert to opportunities that meet their re-created or reimagined work activities to achieve the bigger organizational goals. We explore task crafting further in chapter 3.

The third dimension of job crafting, relational crafting, has to do with changing the relational character of the job by changing either the quality or number of interactions with others at work. For example, an employee in a customer service role may have the opportunity to turn a one-time buyer into a lifelong fan of the product. This would entail going above and beyond the basic requirements of the job to ensure that the customer was satisfied. Another example is an administrative assistant who takes on additional tasks, such as training new employees, because he or she feels a sense of responsibility for the team's success. This extra effort is not required by the job description but is something that the employee chooses to do to contribute to the team's success.

These examples illustrate how relational crafting can lead to increased job satisfaction by allowing employees to feel as though they are making a difference in the lives of others. This is closely linked to task crafting because it creates meaningful relationships with other colleagues. Relational crafting begins as a decision that emerges from reconceptualizing the purpose of work relationships. The focus is still on achieving set objectives; however, the employee can adopt a different approach to work relationships. Relational crafting alters the nature of relationships with colleagues in a more explicit way, with purpose and stronger motivation in mind. This step change aligns with the rise of collaborative and project-based work. By collaboration, we mean working with others to achieve a common objective. The objective, in this case, is the organization's overall objectives, that is, the answer to the question "why do we do the things we do?" Employees may not have a ready answer for this question as it lies at the very core of the organization's operations. However, by working with others, employees cocreate an experience within the larger whole as the ship is steered toward its ultimate destination, that is, its reason for being. The relationships built during these interactions shift from transactional to transformational, with employees working toward shared outcomes. For example, why should you change the number of interactions and the quality of interactions with others at work? The reason is that it helps you to create a stronger sense of purpose for your work. In turn, this can lead to increased job satisfaction and motivation.

There is a finite amount of time that can be spent at work. Because time is a limited resource, employees need to think carefully about how their time is utilized so that they are able to achieve their goals for each workday. Then there are certain work relationships that are directly connected to the achievement of tasks. It makes sense for employees to cultivate such relationships and to build stronger collaboration with colleagues. Other relationships may not be task-related but may serve other purposes, such as fostering an amiable work climate and strengthening cohesion in the wider organization. A purely instrumental approach to relating with other colleagues is ethically problematic and may be frowned upon as manipulative. The instrumental approach says, "I don't really need you for you; I need you so I can get what I want." This approach treats people as a means to an end and does not augur well for building cohesive and collaborative work relationships. Relational crafting, however, allows employees to create meaningful relationships even when those relationships are not directly concerned with accomplishing tasks. That is, we become intentional about how we relate with others, and we nurture those relationships. This is possible because the employee reframes how colleagues are seen. Research by Robin Dunbar, an Oxford evolutionary psychologist, reveals that we are able to hold meaningful relationships with up to 150 people.[10] This finding contrasts with the huge number of friends we may have acquired on social media platforms such as Facebook or Instagram, or the number of Twitter followers. Accordingly, relational crafting becomes an intentional shaping of meaningful relationships that is beyond the casual connections we see on social media. Let's suppose Dunbar is correct. In that case, employees should consider who forms their networks at work, and particularly who can help meet the organization's objectives, because of humans' limited capacity to sustain meaningful relationships beyond the golden 150 number. We explore relational crafting further in chapter 4.

Research on job crafting, which typically focuses on employees, already highlights considerable positive outcomes that help lower employee attrition rates, including increased job satisfaction, organizational commitment, and adaptability in the face of change.[11] Redesigning roles can lead to improved ability to handle time pressures and increased responsibility, and help employees access supportive resources to cope with the demands or uncertainties of their jobs (e.g., interpersonal conflict, role ambiguity). Job crafting is a way that a much broader group than the individual can achieve these goals and so would be expected to reduce stress levels and exhaustion and minimize the likelihood of burnout, all of which are associated with higher employee turnover. As organizations face high turnover costs, which are approximately four times the salary of middle managers and ten times that of senior leaders, finding ways to retain talent makes business sense.

Job crafting is also a powerful tool to facilitate development. For example, tasks and relationships can be added to roles to broaden

horizons and experience, and elements of the position can be reimagined to create a different purpose. Job crafting serves to support workers throughout their life cycle by facilitating the transitions that mark
career progress from early-stage development to retirement, making
the process more sustainable by enabling them to protect their well-
being and avoid burnout. Given the significance of these findings, we
draw on data from a previous study in which structured interviews
were conducted with one thousand business leaders and two thousand
of their workers around the world (67.1 percent from North America
and 32.9 percent from the UK and Australia) for evidence of the useful-
ness of job crafting and to put together guidance for managers wish-
ing to encourage their team members to job craft.[12] The study assessed
each organization's readiness for job crafting and identified the culture,
process, and people factors that make efforts to implement job crafting successful. Because it's a bottom-up approach, job crafting can be
entirely successful only if it's supported at, and encouraged by, all levels of management. Where instances of such commitment existed, the
research found that job crafting

- *Improved well-being:* 92 percent of the interview participants who
  engaged in crafting after the pandemic experienced a more satisfying
  work-life balance and increased personal satisfaction. This improved
  sense of well-being led to a 29 percent decrease in stress levels.
- *Improved collaboration:* 67 percent of participants who engaged in job
  crafting felt inspired to move out of their comfort zones and engage
  in active cooperation with other colleagues, leading to a more connected workforce.
- *Increased productivity:* 77 percent of participants who engaged in job
  crafting were more productive at work than those who did not.
- *Strengthened loyalty:* Staff turnover within organizations utilizing
  crafting decreased by 29 percent because those seeking promotion
  looked internally first before pursuing roles externally. Active job
  crafters were more likely to stay put and adjust their roles than to
  move to another organization.

But the real question is, given the obvious benefits discussed, how do you encourage employees to pursue job crafting? The practice must be implemented and managed effectively. To this end, crafting must align with both the employee's and the company's goals. That's because there are three main forms job crafting adjustments can take. The research found that most crafting (76 percent) occurring post-pandemic altered tasks rather than relationships or cognition. This is because home-based work and the ensuing videoconference fatigue have destroyed traditional ways of interacting with others at work, such as water cooler discussions and coffee bar chat. It's also hard at the moment to alter one's perceptions of the purpose and meaning of work, insofar as many people throughout the world are experiencing cognitive overload. Managers, then, need to make special interventions to help. A four-element framework for managers to make job crafting possible was thus recommended:

1. *Provide employees with permission to craft.* It's vital that employees have the autonomy and empowerment to adapt their job descriptions and responsibilities, thus creating work that is personally meaning-ful, engaging, and satisfying. While this does not entail changing the job description or role per se, it does involve the employee hav-ing the freedom to choose the means to the end.

2. *Provide employees with a psychological safe space to craft.* By creating an environment where employees feel comfortable and are not ridi-culed for sharing innovative ideas, they can experiment with new methods and potentially even make mistakes without fear of judg-ment or scrutiny. To enhance the impact and implementation of employees' ideas, managers should ask employees the right ques-tions, such as "What are your strengths that the team can count on you for?" "What are some of your strengths that are currently unde-rutilized by the team?" "What is a recent mistake that you made, but that you learned a lot from?" and "What skills or areas of improve-ment are you trying to develop?"

3. *Provide employees with the tools they need to craft.* Employees need autonomy, control, trust, and decision latitude over their workloads. Managers are often concerned that crafting provides employees with an excuse to drop their primary tasks and responsibilities, not realizing that crafting, if done well, aligns with employees' strengths, motives, and values. For example, managers can allow some employee discretion in designing day-to-day work and task activities around the fulfillment of work goals; the key is striking a balance between alignment and empowerment so that managers become enablers rather than enforcers. The study found that managers who remove impediments rather than create them through bureaucratic practices can ensure employees do not misuse crafting to drop their tasks and responsibilities but rather use it as an intervention that enhances the achievement of their daily goals.

4. *Provide employees with sufficient freedom to craft.* This includes ensuring that employees' workloads are realistic, that employees have clear role boundaries, and that they have protected time to craft. For example, managers can actively provide on-job time for crafting by allocating an hour or two, daily or weekly, for employees to think out of the box, thus creating more capacity to craft. While doing so may create operational challenges, it facilitates employees developing task, relational, and cognitive landscapes that bring meaning to work.

In subsequent chapters, we explore each of these four elements of the framework in greater detail with case studies and examples highlighting how each element can be achieved in organizations. In the immediately following chapter we take up the three dimensions of job crafting—cognitive crafting, task crafting, and relational crafting.

2 Cognitive Crafting, Task Crafting, and Relational Crafting

This chapter dives into the specifics of job crafting by addressing its three main dimensions: task crafting, relational crafting, and cognitive crafting. Operationally, individuals engaged in task crafting can choose to do fewer, more, or different tasks, depending on various contextual elements; individuals engaged in relational crafting can change the quality and number of interactions with others; and individuals engaged in cognitive crafting can change their perception of the meaning of work. The examples referenced in this chapter illustrate in practical terms how these goals are achievable, and we provide steps toward that end.

Concepts of Cognitive Crafting, Task Crafting, and Relational Crafting

Cognitive, task, and relational crafting as essential dimensions of job crafting have been of interest to researchers since the early 2000s. The argument for these three dimensions characterizes work in terms of the activity to be executed, the human network within which the activity is undertaken, and the mental conditioning of the individual undertaking the activity. In other words, the person doing the task is intricately connected to other persons who are involved in their own tasks but whose activities and relations are intertwined in ways that deliver a bigger goal, that of the organization. This framing is particularly important for managers of contemporary organizations, for whom collaborative work is fundamental to their role.

This understanding of the dimensions of job crafting entertains a view of the organization as unitary, with all units and all workers working together seamlessly to achieve organizational objectives. It assumes a common goal to which all members of the organization subscribe as they perform their tasks, relate to others in their networks, and cognitively position themselves for delivering their given tasks. It is as though the organization were a machine in which every part contributed to the overall outcome. Some may take this critical stance as organizations are not machines with perfectly functioning parts. As highlighted in the previous chapter, viewing organizations as a gathering of different actors, groups, functional units, departments, team, hierarchies, and so on is a necessary precondition for understanding task, relational, and cognitive crafting as part of job crafting. This is not to say that the organization is one big conflict zone. Of course, alliances emerge or are formed based on some kind of shared purpose, even if that is only a perceived commonality. Our contention is that, even in those alliances, cognitive, task, and relational crafting can occur. In the following discussion we delve into these three dimensions of job crafting. We focus on the individual manager involved in job crafting and what that person's approach to job crafting means for the workplace.

Cognitive Crafting

The first dimension of job crafting is cognitive crafting, which concerns shaping the purpose and meaning of an individual's work. While task and relational crafting operate in the observable domain—one can observe what a person does and to whom that person relates in the workplace—cognitive crafting is not easily observable. This is because cognitive crafting takes place in the mind and worldview of the individual. Cognitive crafting addresses gaps between what a person does and how that activity connects to a wider, meaningful purpose. Humans in general work to earn a living, to pay bills and meet basic needs such as food, shelter, and clothing. However, some types of work may carry greater meaning for the individual worker in that they fulfill a higher purpose for the individual, beyond earning income. For example, work in the health care and charity sectors often aims to provide support for and improve the health and well-being of members of society, including the physically or mentally challenged, as well as all other vulnerable groups. Individuals who engage in work of this type are likely to derive satisfaction from making a positive difference to society, which provides a form of personal fulfillment. While the routine aspects of such work keep organizations going, the purpose of the work has symbolic meaning for both workers and beneficiaries. Sometimes this symbolic value is evident in how language is used to define roles and responsibilities, or in the value workers bring. For example, workers in the UK National Health Service (NHS) during the COVID-19 pandemic were frequently referred to as *front-line,* a term more often associated with military personnel during war situations. This term was commonly used during the pandemic to underscore the high level of risk these workers were constantly exposed to and to elevate their contributions to parallel those of soldiers on the battlefield. Both clinical and nonclinical personnel were described as front-line workers because they provided essential services during a national health crisis. For health care workers, the high-risk conditions during the pandemic highlighted the symbolic dimension of their role at individual, societal, and national levels. This is an example of work serving both a functional and a symbolic purpose.

For many workers, the initial or main driver of work seeking might be functional. Government concerns with unemployment statistics are geared toward ensuring that people can earn their livelihoods. Recent research, however, has shown the increasing importance of meaningfulness in work, beyond rewards, compensation, and advancement.[1] At the managerial level, having responsibility for others provides opportunities to expand how work roles and responsibilities are conceived, beyond what is specified in employment contracts. Managers may engage in cognitive crafting to find purpose and meaning in their work and, as a consequence, have organizational impact through greater engagement and commitment.

The absence of meaning reduces a job to mechanical tasks uncon-nected to a wider purpose. This disconnect is often found as one of the dysfunctionalities of the classic bureaucratic organizational structure, where groups and teams operate within silos that do not share informa-tion or goals, or even *talk* to each other. The danger posed by such a narrow focus on tasks is that individuals and teams may be overtaken by goal displacement, where the focus shifts from the wider organi-zational purpose of a task to the achievement of process accuracy, often described as engaging in a *box-ticking exercise*. Such disconnects create conditions that bring about the need for cognitive crafting. In the absence of job enrichment or task variety, monotony can set in on jobs that involve routinized tasks because humans are not machines hard-wired to do the same thing repeatedly. There is a point at which successive labor inputs result in reduced productivity, or diminishing marginal returns. Simply put, as an individual repeats the same task over and over, the ensuing boredom can lead to increasing disengage-ment.[2] In fact, studies show other negative outcomes from highly routinized, repetitive tasks, such as substance abuse, stress, poor health, and low performance.[3] In this context, individuals could begin to ques-tion the meaning of their work.[4] Research suggests that cognitive job crafting increases productivity because it empowers individuals to transform their work into a more ideal job, one that utilizes more of their skills and abilities.[5]

Cognitive job crafting can also be a response to challenges asso-ciated with work over which an individual has little or no control. Within the framework of such limitations, a person could engage in reflective thinking to craft meaning for his or her role as a rebalancing strategy.[6] This suggests that actions by managers could lead individuals to question what they do and begin a search for meaning. Such actions include taking employees for granted, giving people pointless work to do, treating people unfairly, overriding people's judgment, and so on. The search for meaning might also be triggered by an incongruence between a person's values and the organization's values. For example, a clash between an organization's focus on quantitative measures of productivity (profitability) and a manager's focus on more qualitative aspects of work output can be expected to create tension and cognitive disequilibrium, prompting a turn to cognitive job crafting. In this situation, cognitive job crafting would help a manager articulate how he or she approaches the task and the means taken to achieve a desired end, despite seeming incompatibility with the organizational framework. For managers, it is also important to communicate to direct reports and other members of the organization that *what they do matters*. In this way, managers can help individual workers find meaning in work. Managers also have the capability to destroy the meaningfulness of work for employees, thus potentially triggering cognitive job crafting by employees.

Cognitive job crafting could also occur where a person identifies with the organizational purpose. In teams where managers create a positive work culture and an atmosphere where all employees are valued irrespective of their role, it is easy to have organizational members who redefine the purpose of their work and identity. A good illustration of cognitive crafting is the likely fictional story of the NASA janitor who described his work to President John F. Kennedy as "helping put a man on the Moon." The janitor had a different perception of his own identity and work and how those connected with the wider, lofty organizational goal and purpose. Underutilization of an individual's skills and abilities in a given role may also create the need to make sense of the job and expand the range of activities such that the overall effort is steered in a meaningful direction. In this sense, the individual has the capacity to do more and therefore is potentially able to make a positive difference, which links to the sense of self and the value that can be offered in the workplace beyond formally assigned job tasks.

To cognitively craft therefore involves a reimagining of the self at work and a location of that self in a goal-oriented framework that goes beyond the specific mundane tasks that are routinely performed. Whereas the example of the NASA janitor is striking, it does not mean a sheer change of name for one's role. For example, a bin man who calls himself a sanitary engineer is not necessarily doing cognitive crafting, nor is a street beggar who introduces himself as a freelance fund collector. What cognitive crafting involves is an identification of one's work with a sense of mission and letting that shine through one's work ethic. The airline industry is known for its stringent training for staff and cabin crew. For instance, it's been reported that United Airlines took its staff through compassion training in 2018 in order to improve customer service ratings after several dissatisfied customers posted online videos that went viral.[7] Another report tells of the bizarre way the cabin crew of some airlines are taught to smile by holding chopsticks across their lips for several minutes.[8] Whereas training of this sort may be necessary, cognitive job-crafting strategies might better help these workers deliver the outcomes of compassionate service and smiling that are sought.

As a manager, you can encourage cognitive crafting in your organization by using stretch goals. Stretch goals are Moon-shot desires that are aspirational in nature. They are not immediately achievable with measurable outcomes, but they inspire purpose and drive the individual toward achieving it. President Kennedy's famous "we are going to place a man on the Moon" did not place Americans on the Moon at the time he said it but it did inspire hope, faith, and courage in average Americans. On a smaller scale, you can organize stretch goal workshops where you encourage individuals to dream about what they could become in their current roles. If you have the resources, you could offer time-outs for your staff during the workday during which they do whatever they find meaningful but which could potentially make their work more impactful. In your cognitive crafting as a manager, what would you do if you saw your role as one of raising other managers who would be ten times more impactful than you? The freemium Gmail service is Google's main email service, but it came about as a result of one employee, Paul Buchheit. In his words, as reported in *Time* magazine, "I had this idea I wanted to build web-based email. I worked on it for a couple of weeks and then got bored. One of the lessons I learned from that was just in terms of my own psychology, that it was important that I always have a working product."[9] Staff at Google are allowed 20 percent of their work hours to experiment with their own ideas or anything that is not part of their official work tasks. Although it is widely believed that Buchheit created Gmail during this 20 percent time, Gmail actually became an official project he was tasked to do.[10] It was a dream he had before joining the company. Now that dream would somehow be achieved. Through cognitive crafting, Buchheit saw his role as going beyond being an engineer or Google's twenty-third employee in 1999. He had gotten bored working on this idea of an email system, but in his words, his "own psychology" had a role to play in the eventual success of Gmail. As mentioned earlier, cognitive crafting happens at the level of the mind. It may not be observable to others but is instantiated in the individual whose mind is actively crafting his or her job. Buchheit would pursue his dream of developing an email although Google's main business was in the search domain. Cognitively, he considered his personal success to be linked to the development of the email system. It was as though he wanted to prove a point to himself, not compete with others in the company. He mentally took the job as accomplishing something for himself but also beyond himself by creating a product that would be unique to Google's own portfolio of products and services. Buchheit pursued a lofty goal in Google, but in the end, the proof was in the pudding when Gmail was launched on April Fools' Day of 2004. Only this time it wasn't a prank.

Task Crafting

Task crafting entails a redefinition of task boundaries. This may sound disingenuous because the manager is recruited for a task whose scope is often predefined. The expectations of the manager's role may often include a tacit understanding that the original scope of work will be expanded as part of managerial capacity expansion and the firm's commitment to growth. This ever-expanding scope of work that managers often must deal with further supports the need to task craft as a manager. This will allow the manager to create conditions for employees to also task craft, which ultimately produces an environment in which people can creatively renegotiate the boundaries of their given tasks. Additionally, task crafting as a manager means that managers have greater room to delegate various aspects of what they do, potentially allowing others to take on leadership responsibilities.

Task crafting is particularly crucial in the digital era, where various tasks can be done with the click of a mouse or are fully automated. From F. W. Taylor's 1911 treatise on management, which sought to rationalize work tasks, to the digital era, in which algorithms execute work tasks, the pursuit of efficiency has driven management practices. This has occurred even though some of the decisions made by managers and intended to make work tasks more efficient have resulted in catastrophic firm losses and bankruptcies. For example, FoxMeyer Drugs' implementation of enterprise resource planning (ERP) systems ultimately resulted in bankruptcy because the cost of implementation continued to spiral upward. The US Internal Revenue Service's project on taxpayer compliance took ten years to complete, resulting in an unanticipated cost of $50 billion to the taxpayer. Hershey Foods' implementation of ERP systems failed, leading to distribution problems and a loss of 27 percent of the company's market value. There are many more examples.[11]

We do not take a reductionist view and attribute these outcomes to one cause. In fact, they could be due to process failure, that is, an overrun of budgets or time constraints; or to correspondence failure, that is, failure to meet the objectives set for the implementation of the efficient technological system; or to interaction failure, that is, poor user acceptance and satisfaction; or to expectations failure, or failure of the implemented system to meet a particular stakeholder group's expectations.[12] Nonetheless, the pursuit of efficient working models has precipitated a turn to technological systems that either simplify work tasks or execute tasks without human intervention. Task crafting in the digital era is thus implicitly built into the work of individuals as they use contemporary technologies. For instance, firms can now avoid assigning personnel to the drudgery of a routinized task such as answering online queries by building a chatbot to do this work autonomously. The human worker is not a machine that is capable of endless mechanical and routinized tasks—a long-standing criticism of Fordist scientific management approaches to work, which have also been criticized for the deskilling of the workforce.

Accordingly, contemporary digital technologies in the workplace mean that task crafting must have intentionality if it is to yield its full benefits. As highlighted in chapter 1, task crafting does not mean changing the work contract or a worker's position. It is a reconceptualization of the various tasks that together form part of a manager's day-to-day job. If, for example, you are the manager of a school, are you raising future leaders or are you simply leading a school? In the case of the former (explained in more detail under cognitive crafting), you would examine your daily tasks for the degree to which they contribute to educating and nurturing future leaders. It might mean taking on new tasks that are not necessarily spelled out in your work contract, or letting others do tasks that were previously under your direct control. This might result in delegating all those tasks that do not directly contribute to raising future leaders but remain important to your school. Recent research by University of Reading faculty shows the importance of delegation as a skill that managers must *have* as part of their practice and not only as what they *do* among other tasks.[13] The study shows that managers who inspire trust and empowerment are those who habitually delegate tasks. When you task craft, you redraw the boundaries of your work, entrusting others with what was uniquely your task, thereby empowering the delegatee.

Additionally, the introduction of various artificial intelligence (AI) technologies into work processes means that the nature of managerial work is rapidly changing. If the managerial task is conceived of as entailing planning, scheduling, monitoring, control, and so on, that view is now obsolete: AI applications easily perform these tasks and issue forecasts for better management. As a result, managers already are in a situation requiring task crafting, even if they prefer the status quo. It is no longer a question of whether the manager must task craft, it is a question of how to task craft. In our view, task crafting is a given in contemporary organizations. Its intricate connection to delegation means that you can be more proactive in initiating specific changes to your work that make it more meaningful to you and your employees. This might require you to innovate in a specific way with regard to your tasks. We call this *process innovation* as it is indeed more about process.[14] Whereas innovation has often been synonymous with the appearance of new products and services or with technological advances, task crafting takes process innovation as its goal. This involves, first, *decomposing each task into its constituent parts*. Doing so allows you as manager to have a broad understanding of what your tasks actually involve. It brings to the fore what was hidden while making prominent what is really useful. The process of task decomposition also enables you to see what tasks depend on external stakeholders. By decomposing tasks into their parts you can more strategically align your efforts with the time and resources available and delegate other parts to be executed without your direct supervision. A task decomposition activity might look like figure 2.1 on your flipchart (figure 2.1).

Diagramming task decomposition visually on an electronic or physical whiteboard or a flipchart can help you identify clearly and label elements of the decomposed tasks and subtasks that require significant external stakeholder involvement or participation. You can use different shapes to make the different decomposed tasks stand out. For example, those involving external stakeholders could have porous borders that represent external inflow/outflow. Those subtasks that can be delegated could be oval or any other shape that helps you quickly identify them as delegatable tasks, and so on.

Second, task crafting entails *examining the work processes that each task fits into or leads to*. This involves stepping back to gain a panoramic

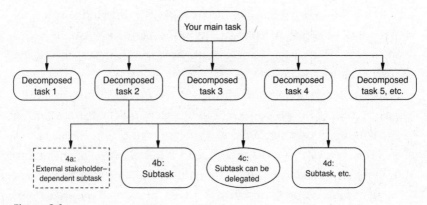

Figure 2.1
A task decomposition chart.

view of how your tasks fit into your bigger assignment as a manager. You must not lose sight of this important goal. You don't want to get lost in the details of what tasks you do and miss the bigger picture of why you are there as a manager. We agree with Simon Sinek, who in his book, *Start with Why,* suggests we should always ask why we do what we do.[15] Consequently, in examining the work processes that each task fits into or leads to, you draw out the sequence of your task flows, asking at each stage *why* you do what you do and *why* one task leads to another. This process engages your reflective self as you map out the flow of your tasks. To do this well, use your task decomposition diagram to capture every task in a task sequence chart. The sequence chart of your tasks will also help you see more clearly what can be taken out of the work process without significantly affecting the final outcome of your work. This means you can redraw the boundaries of scope of your work, crafting it in ways that are unique to you and deliver superior value to you and your business. Your second stage of examining how each task fits into or leads to another might look like what is shown in figure 2.2, though there is enormous variability.

Task sequencing offers visual clarity as to what comes first and what makes logical sense. You may in the process observe gaps or redundancies in your work, in which case you can take steps to address those issues. Recently we posed a challenge to a group of managers at a Fortune 500 company as they implemented a new technology. They were worried

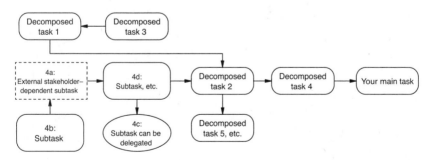

Figure 2.2
Task sequencing chart.

about employee buy-in, but we thought that as managers, they should start with their own work tasks, and we asked them to reexamine their own roles in light of the implementation of the technology. Task decomposition and task sequencing of managerial activities soon showed what could become potential pain points for employees. Those points had nothing to do with the usually blamed "employee resistance." Rather, they showed up as tasks and processes that could be realigned or simply removed to improve the work experience for the managers and their employees. This is an exercise that you can do as a reflective manager, either alone or with a group of employees to help them in task crafting. The benefit is an intentional environment that is built in a way that allows people to do what is meaningful for them. In the process they are empowered to make decisions about their work and to take on the work of others, perhaps becoming delegates for you as you offer them what you have already identified as delegatable in your own task crafting. The final stage in task crafting involves continuous review as new tasks emerge and your business expands (or perhaps shrinks) in response to the challenges of the external market and environment.

Relational Crafting

Relational crafting entails taking ownership of reshaping work relationships and expanding the boundaries of such relationships beyond the expectations associated with formal reporting lines or team structures.[16] This can be done either through the quality or the number of interactions. The quality of relationships speaks to deepening social relations in the workplace and is underpinned by increased knowledge of others through in-depth interactions, the sharing of both work-related and non-work-related information, and reciprocity. Like task crafting, relational crafting is an intentional approach to redefining the broad limits around whom an individual relates to in the workplace and how. By reprioritizing relationships in the workplace, relational crafting aims to create a meaningful balance for the manager between work aims and objectives and personal goals, needs, and values, while taking into consideration available time and the value offered to others. In face-to-face contexts, relational crafting can be expressed through both formal and informal engagements such as work meetings, informal lunches, or chats over coffee. It may also include extending relationships beyond the workplace setting.

What drives relational crafting? A number of push factors may create conditions for relational crafting. These include the needs of the manager and his or her personal values, beliefs, and experiences in the workplace. Where a manager identifies a person with the skills or abilities that meet his or her work-related needs, the manager may try to develop a relationship with that person. For example, if a manager identifies an employee in an adjacent department who has skills that could be drawn on, there is a natural interest in making connections with such an employee or colleague and nurturing that relationship. This requires some degree of openness to learning by the manager as the new relationship is not defined by organizational rules and reporting structures. It is also worth noting that the newly formed relationship is more likely to be successful if the employee or colleague is open to working with the manager and can offer value. The conceptualization of relational crafting must therefore take into account the willingness of the other party to enter into a relationship and the change in power relations. This observation underscores the mutuality and reciprocity that characterize effective relationships in the workplace.

At times an individual may be driven by personal values either to enter into new relationships or to gain some distance from others. If a manager observes teams that exhibit negativity and create a toxic environment in the organization, she may decide to distance herself from such colleagues. If they are in the same work group, she may limit interactions to work-related issues only and communicate unavailability for non—work-related activity. Conversely, if a manager observes other colleagues with whom she shares a work ethic, values, and ideals, there is an impetus to draw closer and establish closer relationship ties.

In addition to push factors, pull factors can also drive relational crafting. Helpfulness, supporting junior colleagues, or bringing a team-based perspective to work are some values that can pull people together in the workplace. For example, a manager may decide to create new programs or workplace initiatives to support employees or colleagues in particular areas. Such altruistic acts often are outside the scope of the individual's primary role and may be time-consuming. However, a manager may see the self as occupying a particular role based on the manager's values, and then engage in activities that express that role. For instance, a manager may take on a volunteer mentoring role for employees outside her formal team. Informal sponsor-protégé relationships are other examples of relational crafting based on needs or values.

Negative experiences at work may also be triggers for relational crafting and could result in an individual either expanding or contracting relationship boundaries at work. Where there are unmet expectations from senior colleagues or violations of the psychological contract, conditions for relational crafting are created.[17] Similarly, if an individual feels unmotivated, is unchallenged in a current role, or has underutilized skills, that person may create avenues to use such dormant skills. This may involve creating new relationships and focusing on efforts to connect with potential beneficiaries of those skills. In all such cases, relational crafting entails expanding or contracting one's relationship network or adjusting the intensity of relationships in a way that aligns with the individual's goals, needs, and values to achieve a balance that allows meaningful work.

Relational crafting requires an investment of time and resources. It is not enough to map out one's current and planned relationship network. There must be an understanding of both the potential value new alliances might bring and the value the manager can offer to achieve a mutually beneficial relationship. After that, the manager must make an intentional investment of time and resources in building the relationship. Because working hours are limited, it may be necessary to develop potential relationships outside formal working hours and to seek nonwork opportunities to gradually build these relationships.

An essential element of relational crafting is communication, without which the value in relationships cannot be realized. Communication can take place in face-to-face encounters or through a technologically mediated medium such as the telephone, email, videoconferencing (Zoom, Slack, Google Meets, Microsoft Teams), or other mobile phone applications. There are benefits and drawbacks to both approaches to communication; however, significant traction can be gained from face-to-face interactions early in a new relationship, even if subsequent encounters are conducted on technology platforms.[18] Research shows that face-to-face engagements allow participants to benefit from non-verbal cues, which enrich and deepen communication.[19] These meetings are essential for building trust or communicating empathy in relationships. Because humans are social animals, face-to-face encounters represent a natural form of engagement that can temper or prevent alienation from others.

In an increasingly technologized world characterized by flexible working conditions and collaborative technologies, however, it is important to be aware of the potential downside to the use of technology in manager-employee relationships.[20] Possible negative effects of relying on technology for communication include isolation, exclusion, surveillance, and self-censorship.[21] These issues can have an impact on the quality of relationships, particularly when the manager is job crafting in a technological work domain. To manage these unintended consequences, research suggests three steps to consider:

- *Foster social connection.* This step argues the need to intentionally craft relationships through meaningful social interactions, even if that means organizing informal gatherings using collaborative technologies if your employees are dispersed and working remotely. For example, work colleagues and employees could be brought together for a virtual coffee hour and non-work-related conversation.

- *Prevent exclusion through meaningful participation.* Employees can be encouraged to participate in specific collaborative events in order to prevent situations conducive to the formation of in-groups and out-groups. Such events might involve training sessions to further employees' knowledge of a specific work domain.

- *Lead with transparency when it comes to surveillance.* Policies should be in place that make clear what data are collected on your employees as they engage with the technologies in the organization. Employees should have the right to choose what and how their personal data will be used by the company. To lead with transparency is to be as open as possible in aligning your actions with your espoused values as an organization.[22]

In the postpandemic workplace, where relationships are formed or sustained through collaborative technologies, technological savviness becomes important to you as a manager. You don't have to be a digital native or Gen Zer to master the technologies available for work. (We find generational categories unhelpful because the rapid pace of digital innovation means everyone will have to work to grasp its potential.) In contemporary organizations, the manager's work requires the use of digital technologies, and relational crafting will therefore involve leveraging various technologies to achieve a specific goal. We are all "digital immigrants" as we adopt digital innovations and new uses of technology in the workplace. To relationally craft in this era means understanding the appropriate role of technology as you build relationships with colleague managers or employees. As shown in figure 2.3, for example, your relationship with employees might have to transition from the traditional manager-employee hierarchy to a manager-collaborator relationship.

In a manager-employee relationship such as depicted in figure 2.3, transitioning from point A to point B means reconceptualizing who the employee is to you as a manager. In their book *A World Gone Social*, Coine and Babbitt decry the obduracy of hierarchies in contemporary organizations and call for flatter organizational organograms to compete in a world where it is Silicon Valley–style management practices

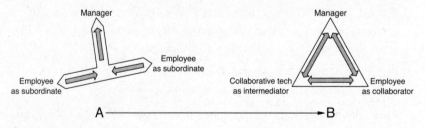

Figure 2.3
Transitioning from a manager-employee to a manager-collaborator relationship.

that focus on delivering impressive results quickly.[23] Although these ideas offer value, our own research shows that hierarchies often exist alongside flatter organizational forms within the same business.[24] In fact, even in those organizations where the organogram portrays a flat organization, there are still some emergent, perceived, or implicit hierarchical forms. As a result, you are likely to engage in relational job crafting within already established hierarchies. Our combined experience in researching and working with managers in various organizations across the world suggests that in relational crafting, you are better positioned when you transition from treating your employees as subordinates to relating to them as collaborators. Management scholar Joseph Rost argues vehemently against what he calls a "hopelessly irredeemable" conceptualization of employees as subordinates or followers.[25] This is particularly the case as work in the postpandemic world is largely accomplished using collaborative technologies, generally platforms on which managers and employees interact in executing their various tasks. The very architecture of the technology means that a hierarchical positioning as manager is irrelevant if you wish to engage with your colleagues or your employees. It is thus useful to relationally craft your job in ways that see employees as collaborators who are on the same level as you and possess something to offer, not as subordinates waiting to receive orders from you. Job crafting through reshaping work relationships in this new way empowers the team, increases trust, and extends your influence as you gain more from your employees' creativity.

As shown in the examples, all three dimensions of job crafting are interrelated. In particular, we see the key role of cognitive crafting in framing decisions around task and relational crafting. Underpinning all three dimensions of job crafting is the idea that crafting is a response to gaps between what is being done in a work role and an individual's contextual conditions. The next chapter considers organizational and individual readiness for job crafting as key contextual factors.

3   Readiness for Job Crafting

Both organizational and individual readiness are needed for job crafting. Factors discussed in this chapter pertinent to organizational readiness include process, people factors, and some bottom-up approaches that can be deployed to prepare organizations for job crafting. For individual readiness, an assessment of strengths and weaknesses should be undertaken, to include workplace opportunities and limitations, the availability of supportive networks, and the strength of personal values. The chapter also highlights the importance of employee buy-in and considers the potential challenges that may arise when aligning employee job crafting with organizational goals. Case studies are introduced to show the practicalities of job crafting and consequent implications for line managers. We end this chapter by listing some preconditions for successful job crafting.

Organizational Readiness for Job Crafting

Job crafting works successfully when there are facilitating contextual conditions, including all the conditions that lead to organizational and individual readiness. An individual can make personal decisions to job craft cognitively, relationally, or taskwise. However, these decisions typically are made within the bounds of what the organization allows. This suggests that organizations need to be sufficiently flexible to accommodate job crafting, in particular task crafting, which relates to what is done to achieve organizational goals. While task crafting relies on the ability of the individual to expand or contract the bounds of work done, research indicates that organizational conditions can facilitate or hinder this effort.[1] In a predictable, in-person work context, an individual employee or manager can engage in job crafting by redefining what is done, with whom, and why, within organizational limits. However, various factors can disrupt such frameworks and affect work tasks and work relationships. These factors include changes made as a result of organizational restructuring, acquisitions or mergers, technology and business processes, redundancies, and a wider economic downturn. Such organizational or macro economic changes can in turn precipitate changes in roles, tasks, and work relationships at the individual level, to be met with different degrees of employee adaptability.[2] Radical organizational changes can have profound impacts on individuals and potentially leave them with a need to find meaning.[3] Studies reveal that what leaders do can contribute to employees' sense of meaninglessness, such as when employees feel leaders take them for granted or when they are assigned work they consider meaningless.[4] Change is often a prompt for job crafting to occur, and a flexible organizational approach to work offers a way for workers to make adjustments to the sort of changes noted here.

Modern organizations that allow flexibility in work practices are positioned to reap the benefits of greater productivity and employee satisfaction.[5] Flexibility could apply to work hours, the length of the workday, and the place of work. Flexibility can be built into organizational policies and norms but can also be triggered by external influences. The COVID-19 pandemic and government guidelines for socially distanced work practices were push factors for many organizations to move to more flexible ways of working. With the exception of essential service providers, such as workers in health care, public transit, the press, and law enforcement, many individuals had to switch from in-person work to working from home. There was evidence of increased productivity and innovation, while some employees reported higher performance as a result of the move to flexible working.[6] For some types of work, such as software engineering, information communication, and technology roles, this shift is possible with minimal disruption because systems may already be in place for virtual and remote work. Work in other fields, however, might require significant investment in technological infrastructure for remote performance to be effective. A prime example is education. Primary, secondary, and tertiary education are conventionally delivered in person, but during the pandemic, many schools had to transition to either fully virtual or hybrid forms of delivery. Some traditionally in-person work, such as health care provision, also transitioned to hybrid forms of interaction whereby collaborative technology became the platform for providing services to users. The story is not all rosy: some organizations may be at higher risk of collapse if they are unable to transition to a more flexible and, importantly, virtual operational model. The protracted period of socially distanced work during the COVID-19 pandemic gave organizations the opportunity to reflect on their priorities and reexamine their working arrangements, which ultimately impact individual workers. This ties in with cognitive crafting, where people redefine their role in terms of a purpose they personally connect with and what is meaningful to them. In some cases, some workers left jobs that they found were not contributing to a sense of purpose and meaning. The US Bureau of Labor Statistics indicates that during the pandemic, over 15 million US workers quit their jobs, while a report from Microsoft suggests that 46 percent of the global workforce considered leaving their jobs because they now could choose remote work.[7] Remote working in particular presents a context that more strikingly reveals gaps in the experience of work, particularly in relations with co-workers. By lacking conventional workplace social interactions, remote working creates incentives for workers to seek meaningful connections with work and work colleagues, thereby engaging in relational crafting.

The Role of Process in Job Crafting

While we consider organizational (and individual) readiness for job crafting, we also acknowledge the centrality of process to all job-crafting dimensions, whether task, relational, or cognitive crafting. When we think of a process, it is often in terms of inputs and outputs. A process transforms inputs into outputs, and so a good process is often assumed to yield good outcomes. Managers engage various processes at work to achieve set targets. As illustrated in figure 3.1, *process* can sometimes look like a black box where everything is walled and the walls are non-transparent. Although this may be the experience in some organizations, the seemingly hard boundaries of processes within organizations are actually malleable, depending on what the organization wants to achieve.

Conceptually, it is as though access to what managerial or organizational processes entail were hidden from the view of everyone except a privileged few. In practice, it is true that some processes are not readily visible. For example, the inner workings of a jet engine may not be visible to the passengers embarking on a flight, although it is that same process that takes them to their destination. When it comes to organizational life, processes must not be black boxes. It is when all of the organization's members understand the process that you can ensure adherence. This proposition directly contradicts the popular maxim, "Trust the process."

"Trust the process" gained popularity when it became a maxim touted by fans of the NBA's Philadelphia 76ers (commonly referred to as the Sixers). It was meant to inspire belief in the team at a time when it was not performing particularly well. The fans rallied around the coach and trusted his process of building a formidable team in the expectation that it would yield future results. Whatever the process was, the fans were not aware of the details but believed in it nonetheless. They

Figure 3.1
An illustration of *process* as a black box.

were ready for a change in their team's performance and put their faith in the process, which might as well not have existed because nobody knew the specifics. In job crafting, you should consider what processes employed by your organization could have an impact on your employees' readiness to job craft. Unlike simply trusting the process as the fans of the Sixers did, you may want to identify and make explicit what processes could serve as barriers. Is there process readiness to job crafting in the organization? The question has to do with whether you as a manager are willing to render your processes amenable to change to give your employees the space to job craft. Instead of your processes looking like the illustration in figure 3.1, you might want to work toward a representation of your processes as shown in figure 3.2.

In its first depiction (figure 3.1), *process* has hard boundaries and is rectangular, and its contents are potentially unknown to your employees, much as in the jet engine analogy. In the second depiction of *process* (figure 3.2), it has porous boundaries and is round. Whereas the former makes organizational processes seem rigid and therefore not ready for job crafting, the latter offers malleability, flexibility, and openness to input from others so that it may be made smaller or bigger depending on the inputs. The inputs are also open to contributions from others so that individuals in the organization can freely craft their jobs to deliver the needed output. It is this thinking that underpinned the drive to install remote working processes during the heat of the COVID-19 pandemic, although that was imposed by the authorities. For instance, studies show that 38 percent of jobs in Canada and

Figure 3.2
A new view of *process* for job crafting.

37 percent of jobs in the US that were performed on-site pre-COVID-19 could have been done remotely.[8] Somehow the status quo persisted until government-ordered lockdowns forced a new way of working, and managers had to take action. The lack of flexibility in organizational work processes or the unwillingness of managers to proactively render their work processes malleable led to workers continuing to show up for in-person work when their jobs could, through job crafting, have been done remotely. We are suggesting that it shouldn't take a pandemic to force managers to rethink how work is done. Malleable work processes within the organization can create conditions for your employees to be better prepared for job crafting.

The Role of People-Centric Leadership in Job Crafting

An important thing to remember in organizational life is that the hustle and bustle of work demands, performance targets, and other key performance indicators (KPIs) can make managers lose sight of the single most important thing that makes the organization—its people. Job crafting is all about people making sense of their jobs and crafting those jobs to meet their own aspirations. This means a managerial climate that allows them to do so. We noted earlier the need to be intentional in creating such a climate for your employees. This calls for a certain kind of leadership. By now it should be clear that a top-down approach to leadership does not work if you wish to create an atmosphere that allows your employees to job craft. Top-down leadership is not in itself a bad thing; it has its place in management circles. But it is a leadership style that is directive and seeks results in a unidirectional way. It flows from one person to others, who must comply. This leadership style can often be transactional in its approach so that when directives are followed there is a reward, and when they are not followed punitive measures are taken. Our description may appear to be extreme, but this leadership style in various guises is common to organizations. Again, we note that it has its place, such as in military operations and rescue situations.

In organizational life, however, directive leadership styles can create conditions where employee voice is lost. This is because this leadership style focuses attention on the manager, and everything is all about that person. This leadership style is rooted in heroism, and popular culture has glorified it. Lucy Kellaway, a *Financial Times* columnist, in poking fun at heroic conceptualizations of leadership, wonders why managers seem always to portray themselves as having a thick skin. She argues, and we agree, that managers should also be willing to show their humanity by taking things personally, having their thin skin on display, and connecting with the issues that affect all people, because managers are also people.[9] With this in mind, we stress the need for a new kind of leadership that is not unidirectional but omnidirectional. By omnidirectional we do not mean multidirectional, as these are different conceptualizations. Leadership styles that seem to place the emphasis on you as a manager are unidirectional but can also be multidirectional in nature. The transmission of influence is assumed to be emanating from you, although you know this is not always the case. We illustrate these approaches to leadership in figure 3.3 to offer some clarity.

Unidirectional leadership focuses attention on the leader in an almost militaristic manner. This is often a top-down form of leadership in which the hierarchy dictates what goes on in the organization. Employees become recipients of leadership action and are stuck with what they have to do in their jobs, without avenues for speaking up or questioning orders. Multidirectional leadership similarly keeps the focus on the leader. This leadership style is exemplified by charismatic leaders who are able to extend their reach to various aspects or units

Unidirectional leadership
(Often top-down)

Multidirectional leadership
(Often leader-centric)

Omnidirectional leadership
(Often people-centric)

Figure 3.3
Unidirectional, multidirectional, and omnidirectional leadership.

of the business. However, multidirectionality continues to be a one-way approach, and employees remain unable to freely reexamine their jobs in their own way; it is still about the manager. Omnidirectional leadership shifts the focus from the leader to the group. As a manager, you recognize that you are among people who are as gifted as you, perhaps more gifted. You seek their input in decision-making and allow their voices to be heard. You pay attention to how they do their work and offer suggestions, but also encourage them to challenge your work in turn. Omnidirectionality is people-centric and accepts the fact that you are also influenced by your colleagues, your employees, your stakeholders, and your customers. The French philosopher and anthropologist Bruno Latour would argue that you are even influenced by your electronic devices, software, and other artifacts in your organization in one way or another.[10] This is because all these artifacts also participate in organizational life. If you are holding this book to read, then it has somehow influenced the way you sit, the movements of your hand, what reading glasses you may have put on, where your attention is directed. Influence is therefore omnidirectional, and leadership must be seen this way too if you want to job craft as a manager and lead people in job crafting.

Leadership that creates the atmosphere for job crafting is therefore relational in nature. In a postpandemic era where work is largely intermediated by collaborative technologies, it makes sense to ensure that leadership is people-centric. This is because your employees are now potentially spending significant amounts of time in front of their screens. A 2022 study commissioned by the British firm Vision Direct surveyed two thousand British adults (along with a similar number of US adults) and found they spent 4,866 hours a year staring at screens.[11] This worked out to an average of thirty-four years of their lifetime spent staring at screens. In the US, this figure was much higher—forty-four years of life spent staring at screens. Leadership that does not seek to engage people leaves open the possibility of influence by other factors, which may be unknown. This calls for intentionality in building a people-centric leadership strategy in order to engage your employees in a way that gives them voice so they can speak freely about their jobs in the organization. If your employees are silenced, they will not share their frustrations about their jobs. Neither will they share potential innovations in work processes.

Giving your employees a voice means facilitating the free flow of information in your organization, even if it is only to encourage discussions about what changes they would like to see in their jobs. Leadership scholars James R. Detert and Ethan R. Burris point out that giving employees a voice can empower them to challenge organizational practices, which is exactly what you need in job crafting.[12] Further, giving your employees a voice offers a way for employees to relate to their peers as they speak out, and a way to engage with their managers as they speak up.[13] The decision to speak freely about their jobs is a mark of confidence and trust in you as a manager and in your leadership.[14] It is for these reasons that a manager must be intentional about creating open channels of communication in the organization to encourage the speaking out and speaking up that are crucially needed for job crafting.

This also means being open to voices that convey harsh sentiments. In fact, employees speaking unpalatably about their jobs is a rallying cry for job crafting. William Bridges in his book *Jobshift* opines that what we call a job is dead.[15] In this radical view, the notion of a job is anachronistic, a holdover from the Industrial Revolution when people had a "job" to do. Bridges argues that in the digital era, this concept is no longer sustainable because every worker's job is contingent on the organization's goals, and therefore a job should be managed like that of an external supplier rather than that of the traditional employee. This dark view of jobs calls on you as manager to be sensitive to the needs of your employees, or they might leave you to deliver another "external contract" elsewhere.

Individual Readiness for Job Crafting

The starting point for job crafting is a recognition by the individual that there is a lack of alignment between what an individual does and the individual's skills, desires, and purpose that needs to be addressed.

The previous chapter discussed push and pull factors for job crafting; however, different individuals will respond differently to these factors. Differences in personality and experience come into play, and there are differences in the extent to which people are able to redefine goals and tasks in a way that allows them to engage their underutilized skills. Task crafting requires that individuals be able to reflect on and assess current realities within the framework of their role descriptions and deliverables in the organization. Those who have these abilities can engage in task crafting and, through greater engagement, improve their productivity. This type of employee is good news for you as a manager and exemplifies employeeship. However, others who may be unable to task craft are likely to experience frustration and disengagement from their work. Studies show that employee responses to feeling a lack of purpose range from working to rule, operating in silos, and disengagement, all of which have an impact on productivity.[16]

It is helpful for you as a manager to be aware of these individual differences and to provide support as employees seek to reorganize and develop aspects of their work in ways that provide fulfillment. With respect to relational crafting, you can help employees toward overcoming weaknesses or limitations that prevent them from being able to own and develop their network of social contacts in the workplace. You can become more intentional about recognizing and acknowledging your employees' achievements. This communicates that what your employee does matters and contributes to the organizational goal. When a line manager fails to acknowledge the achievements and successes of workers, it can create a sense of meaninglessness, which in turn may prompt cognitive crafting. At the managerial level, a similar argument can be made for the need for individual readiness for successful job crafting. If you as a manager struggle with a sense of identity and experience misalignment between what you do and where you envision yourself, you are more likely to experience stress at work under these conditions. However, if you have a strong sense of self, then you are more likely to engage in job crafting in line with who you perceive yourself to be. Unfortunately, cognitive crafting may not always be in the direction of organizational goals but geared more toward the individual's goals. To job craft successfully, therefore, an individual (whether manager or subordinate) needs to have clear personal values that act as an anchor for giving meaning to what they do, a strong sense of identity that allows them to define fulfillment in more personal terms, and a support group that reinforces their identity and celebrates their achievements and successes.

Understanding Opportunities for Job Crafting

In 2001, in their seminal work, Amy Wrzesniewski and Jane Dutton developed a model of job crafting that delineated the individual motivations that spark job crafting, how opportunities and individual work orientation determine the form job crafting takes, and the most likely organizational and individual effects.[17] This framing of the phenomenon underscores the importance of contextual factors for successful job crafting and the dynamic nature of job crafting. Opportunities for job crafting could arise from organizational growth or expansion that widens the scope of the individual's work beyond contractual terms. When an organization expands as a result of acquiring another business or merging with another organization, the agreement is usually followed by structural changes that create new roles, redefine existing roles, or make other roles redundant. Though a new role already comes with new tasks and relationships, individuals can draw on cognitive and relational crafting to deepen engagement on the job. When existing roles are redefined, there may also be scope for task, relational, and cognitive crafting to utilize any underutilized skills as a result of the changes.

Opportunities for job crafting could also arise through an observation of gaps or problems that call for creative solutions in terms of tasks or relationships. In this regard, a keen observation of qualitative and quantitative data generated in organizations can reveal spaces where improvements can be made. Individuals who voluntarily engage in such reviews of data may be driven by a sense of ownership and commitment to the organization, strong communitarian values, or the desire to make a positive difference as a result of cognitive crafting. Seeing themselves in a different light through cognitive crafting powers their efforts to do much more than their contractual terms stipulate and contribute to the common good of the organization.

As discussed in the previous section, some organizational conditions, particularly ones that create challenges for workers, can also prompt job crafting by the individual. A collaborative and positive relationship with colleagues can strengthen job crafting. A toxic work environment can also lead people to job craft in order to find meaning in an otherwise difficult situation. For example, a poor relationship with a line manager, conflict with other teams, or skill shortages may be push factors driving task, relational, and cognitive job crafting. Reframing those challenges as opportunities allows the individual to take a positive approach to job crafting not only as a coping mechanism for dealing with those challenges but also as a way to put underutilized skills to work and increase work productivity.

Case Study

Haier is an ambitious company that seeks to be the world's foremost brand of consumer white goods. To achieve this global ambition, the company made a series of acquisitions, of which the best known is its acquisition of the American electronics giant GE. Our case study here concerns Haier's 2007 acquisition of Sanyo's refrigerator business.

Sanyo is a Japanese brand, and Haier, a Chinese company, faced the challenge of ensuring brand loyalty, first for its new Japanese employees and second for the general Japanese market, a difficult task for a Chinese company. Twenty years after entering the Japanese market, Haier decided to bring together its sales, R&D, and production units in Japan by building a factory and R&D centers in the country. Additionally, the company hired about seven hundred Japanese staff while also taking over Sanyo's entire white goods business in 2012.

As a Chinese company, Haier faced a culture shift as it sought to expand its business in Japan through the newly acquired Sanyo. This shift involved the understanding that the Japanese operate with traditional bureaucratic structures while Haier favors a decentralized approach to management. Haier had started to revolutionize its own management by adopting a philosophy that focused on empowering employees to take on leadership roles within the company. It saw its acquisition of Sanyo as an opportunity to make a culture change with its new management practice whereby hierarchy would become a thing of the past. The idea was to empower all employees so they could make decisions about their jobs as the company pressed the need for every worker to connect directly with customers. There would no longer be a specific department whose sole aim was customer relations. Instead, every employee would craft their jobs in ways that demonstrated a direct connection to the customer.

The culture shift began when Haier presented what it sought to achieve to all employees. It was left for everyone to reimagine their roles within the company and to examine how they would align what they did with what they now wished to achieve. To do this, managers issued a new system of rewards that contrasted with the system the Japanese were used to. Individuals were to be rewarded on the extent to which they crafted their roles in achieving the aims of the company rather than on the basis of seniority or hierarchy. When Haier acquired Sanyo, 70 percent of Sanyo's employees were older than fifty years and were rewarded on the basis of seniority.

To achieve its aims, Haier decided to bring in younger employees as part of its cultural change. Instead of rewarding workers for longevity in the business, Haier changed the salary structure from Sanyo's previous twelve-month salaries plus a standard four months of bonuses to one of twelve-month salaries with uncapped bonuses. The implication was that an employee could see an overall significant increase in remuneration, which provided motivation for younger workers who wished to earn as much as they could irrespective of how long they had been employed. The new compensation structure also offered a way for individuals to showcase various process innovations that would allow them to fulfill their roles in ways that they saw fit. Instead of waiting for promotion until they were senior employees, workers would be rewarded for their work without any limitations of age or position.

With a newly hired workforce with an average age of twenty-five years, the introduction of a slow bottom-up approach began to turn the tide for the waning Sanyo (now Haier) as the younger employees began crafting their jobs to drive growth by focusing on the customer and establishing relationships that ensured that the voice of the customer would be heard and the customer's needs met, in order to deliver on their performance objectives. Employees were allowed to voice their own concerns about how they wished to run their jobs. Sometimes managers would invite employees to bid for roles of leadership in creating new branches of the company. Suddenly, the atmosphere changed from one in which employees were told what to do, with little room for innovation, to one of expectation that employees would craft their roles in unique ways to achieve their performance targets. Five years into its acquisition of Sanyo, Haier, a Chinese brand, became a household name in Japan.

At the organizational level, managers at Haier decided to create conditions that ensured job crafting. They believed it would take a culture shift to change Sanyo's organizational climate to what they wanted to achieve with the newly acquired company. In doing so, a different kind of leadership was needed. This involved empowering employees to craft their own roles and tieing the remuneration system to the extent to which employees did so. Employee voice was encouraged, thus ensuring omnidirectionality while signaling that the organization was ready for new ways of working. This organizational readiness was needed to ensure individual action from employees. At the individual level, the shake-up of the organizational hierarchy and the hiring of younger employees were intentional acts by managers who wanted to stir older colleagues to move away from old ways of working so they could be free to job craft. Additionally, individuals could redefine their own goals while keeping in mind the bigger vision of closing the employee-customer gap. With organizational readiness creating an opportunity to job craft, employees could develop a strong sense of responsibility for how they reorganized their own jobs to fulfill their aims. They could take ownership of their jobs and creatively develop solutions that would allow them to achieve the set objectives while also being rewarded for it.

Haier made radical changes to embed job crafting into employees' work. This may not be the case for your own organization. You might want to consider incremental approaches that are tailored to your context to create an atmosphere for job crafting in your organization. Haier's unlimited bonus system might not work for you, but some reward system for job crafters in your company might be a small step toward a future giant leap.

Practicalities and Implications of Job Crafting for Managers

As the world of work has become more and more dynamic, with greater volatility, uncertainty, complexity, and ambiguity, organizations have had to develop change competencies that allow them to adjust and stay competitive and relevant. As a manager, therefore, you will benefit from developing an open attitude toward dealing with dynamic work contexts. This dynamism extends to managing your employees and job design, where job crafting represents a modern perspective on job design that puts the individual at the helm. Job crafting appeals to employees because it offers them freedom to redefine what is done, with whom, and for what purpose. However, you as a manager and a key decision-maker in an organization play a significant role in creating conditions for job crafting and ensuring organizational readiness. Some organizations allow employees to spend part of their working hours on pet projects—as a type of task crafting. This approach is organization-driven and provides a defined frame for exercising the freedom to task craft. In such a situation, employees can decide what they want to do within the limited time made available. The underlying assumption is that the pet projects will contribute to organizational productivity. For example, Google allows its employees 20 percent of work time to work on side projects, some of which later may become mainstream and profitable products for the company. The key challenge for you as a manager is to find an alignment between job crafting and the organization's goals.[18] This requires a deeper relationship between you and the teams you supervise to identify potential gaps that may benefit from job crafting. To this end, managers need to understand employees' skill sets, needs, and goals and be able to step in to offer thoughts on how these attributes can contribute to the wider organization. The final decision still lies with the individual; the manager's role is to listen and support. In this way, job crafting will emerge as a way to add value rather than as a coping mechanism for managing challenges on the job. Employees find autonomy empowering, and as a manager you will benefit from motivating your team in this way.

Some employees may need additional support in making bold decisions, and here managers can help them develop acceptance and confidence through delegating tasks that require creative approaches to solving specific problems. Developing these skills will in turn have a multiplier effect for the organization in terms of innovation, productivity, and employee engagement. You can help your employees in the area of relational crafting by expanding their network. You could introduce them to potential collaborators and contacts who could help them achieve their goals. Open discussions with your team could also help you discover what employees' visions, goals, and growth plans are so that you gain an insight into how they see themselves and what that means for your organization. A key benefit of this open approach to managing employees is that you are walking the talk, leading by example and mentoring others to cultivate empowering relationships within the organization. This alignment between organizational talk and action communicates leadership integrity to employees, which results in greater commitment and loyalty. This is valuable for the organization as commitment has been linked to better organizational performance. Additionally, it allows you to approach employee management not from a manipulative angle that treats people as means to an end but in a way that respects individuals. You as a manager will have become the champion of job crafting and will also be able to normalize helping to support individual and organizational readiness for job crafting. All these practicalities manifest an organizational culture that is open to creativity and learning and that values the contributions of members.

Classical management thinking sees management as giving directives to workers within set plans and control mechanisms. More modern approaches emphasize autonomy, empowerment, collaboration, and participation. Job crafting sits within this latter approach, and therefore it is incumbent on you as a manager to examine your ideas of management as they could either hinder or facilitate your ability to support your team with job crafting.

4 Permission to Craft

The first element in the four-element framework of job crafting is understanding the permission structures. Different types of permissions can be granted in organizations. Organizations are social systems, and as such, they are organized around rules and norms. For the organization to function properly, its members need to know what is expected of them and what they are allowed to do. Therefore, organizational structures and cultures together establish what is known as "permission structures," which set forth the limits within which people are allowed to operate. We explore these structures in greater detail in this chapter.

Organizational Culture and Permission to Craft

There are two types of permission structures, explicit and implicit. Explicit permission structures are those that are written down and communicated to employees, for example in an employee handbook or job description. Implicit permission structures are those that are not written down but are understood by employees as they are mediated by the organization's culture and values. An organization's culture and values are the foundation of its identity. They shape how employees interact with each other and with customers, and influence every aspect of the business. From a job-crafting perspective, it is vital that employees have the autonomy and empowerment to adapt their job descriptions and responsibilities, with the goal of creating work that is personally meaningful, engaging, and satisfying to them. The allowance to do so is often embedded in the culture of the organization.

Organizational culture has an impact on whether or not individuals have the flexibility to initiate tasks, projects, and relationships, and whether these efforts are recognized and rewarded. The term *culture* is often narrowly (mis)used to describe an organization's practices. However, culture is much more than what organizations do. It is a multifaceted phenomenon that sits at the heart of an organization's life and comprises values and beliefs, stories, language, artifacts and symbols, rituals and ceremonies, as well as norms and practices. When it comes to organizational culture, what is espoused may differ from what obtains in practice. While an organization may make public statements about its core values and beliefs on its website or in documents, a closer examination of different aspects of the organization, including norms and practices, particularly those that are rewarded, gives a much clearer indication of what is really valued and what is at the heart of its culture. As a result, the real culture is defined by what is valued, which then manifests in observed practices. Definitions of organizational culture frequently fail to adequately capture this value dimension of culture. For instance, Terrence Deal and Allan Kennedy's famous definition of corporate culture as "the way things are done around" here places more emphasis on what is done.[1] However, organizational members are active and not passive agents in shaping their experiences in the workplace. For organizational culture to facilitate job crafting, having shared values is a key means to achieving synergy across the organization. These values include openness to diversity, change, inclusion, and equity. Across different levels of leadership, these values must be understood, shared, and expressed with intentionality. In other words, an organizational culture that allows and rewards creativity, innovative approaches to work, and individual autonomy in the execution of tasks is one that provides a fertile ground for job crafting.

Related to culture is the structure of an organization, which also affects the ease with which individuals are able to engage in job crafting. *Organizational structure* describes the arrangement of relations between the different parts and members of an organization. While there is a formal organizational structure that is found in an organogram and shows the network of formal relationships and obligations in the organization, there is also a more informal, social structure that emerges more organically and often may exist under the radar of the formal HR department. The *social structure* refers to those patterns of work relationships that are often enduring and affect the behavior of individuals in the workplace. These relationships are influential and can make the difference between engagement and disengagement. People typically form bonds and relationships with others who share similar interests or values with them. They could also form relationships with those who offer specific value for the achievement of their work tasks or those to whom value could be given, such as mentees. These relationships rely on the parties recognizing the mutually beneficial nature of the relationship and working toward sustaining it. The informal social structure thus captures relationships in both qualitative and quantitative terms and offers the space for relational crafting, which draws on relations within formal and informal networks. Organizations with vibrant and dynamic social structures present richer opportunities for relational crafting.

A strong culture and set of values can give a firm a competitive advantage, helping to attract and retain the best talent, inspire customer loyalty, and foster innovation. Companies that are clear about their culture and values tend to be more successful than those that are not. Similarly, employees as internal customers who understand and buy into the company's culture and values are more engaged, productive, and loyal, inasmuch as customers who share the same values as the company are also more likely to be satisfied and loyal.

Companies that share the same values as their customers—that is, both internal and external customers—are more likely to be trusted and to develop a loyal following. Satisfied and engaged internal customers (employees) tend to feel that their company genuinely cares about them and is interested in their well-being. In other words, when a company's values align with its customers' values, it builds rapport and trust. This ultimately leads to high levels of engagement, satisfaction, and loyalty. The role of the organization's culture in creating explicit or implicit permission for employees to engage in job crafting is well documented. For instance, the cultural web is a powerful tool for understanding and shaping organizational culture.[2] It can help leaders identify the key elements of their culture and make changes that will have a positive impact on the organization. The culture web consists of six elements: values, norms, beliefs, rituals, symbols, and heroes. Each of these elements plays a role in shaping an organization's culture.

- *Values* are the core beliefs that guide an organization's actions. They are the principles that members of an organization abide by and use to make decisions.

- *Norms* are the expectations that members of an organization have regarding each other's behavior. They define what is acceptable behavior within an organization.

- *Beliefs* are the convictions that members of an organization hold about the way things should be done. They guide an organization's decision-making.

- *Rituals* are the ceremonial activities that members of an organization participate in. They help to reinforce the values and norms of the organization.

- *Symbols* are the physical objects that represent an organization's values and beliefs. They can be anything from the logo of an organization to the building in which it is housed.

- *Heroes* are the individuals who embody an organization's values and norms. They serve as role models for other members of the organization.

In exploring possibilities for job crafting, each of the six components of the culture web serve as cues for employees to understand what is permitted or not within the organization. For instance, in understanding the values of their organization, leaders and employees alike must look beyond an organization's "written values" to discern its "actual values" as manifested in the lived realities of the employees and the actions of the organization. It is also important to understand the end for which values are being practiced. The competing values framework is a tool that can be used to help organizations understand and manage the trade-offs between different organizational values. It can also be used to assess an organization's current state, diagnose problems, and develop strategies for change. The framework is based on the premise that all organizations face trade-offs among four basic values:

- *Efficiency,* which can be summed up as the production of desired outputs with the least amount of inputs (e.g., time, money, resources).
- *Effectiveness,* which refers to the ability to achieve desired outcomes (e.g., goals, objectives) within certain constraints.
- *Flexibility,* or the capacity to adapt quickly to changing conditions or demands.
- *Stability,* or the capacity to maintain predictable patterns of behavior over time.

Each of these values represents a potential source of tension or conflict within an organization. For example, the need for efficiency may conflict with the need for flexibility, or the desire for stability may conflict with the desire to be effective. The competing values framework can be used to help organizations understand and manage these tensions. It can also be used to assess an organization's current state, diagnose problems, and develop strategies for change. When using the competing values framework, it is important to keep in mind that no organization is perfectly balanced. All organizations face trade-offs among different values, and each organization has its own unique mix of values. The goal is not to achieve perfect balance but to understand the trade-offs and make deliberate choices for managing them.

When developing or refining an organization's culture and values, it's important that managers involve employees in the process. After all, they are the ones who will be living and breathing the culture and values every day. Employees can provide valuable insights into what the organization's culture and values should be.

Once an organization's culture and values have been established, it is important to communicate them to everyone in the company. All employees should be aware of what the culture and values are, and how they should be applied in day-to-day work. Leaders need to model the desired behavior and reinforce it through recognition and rewards. Our research has found that organizations that have a strong culture and set of values tend to be more successful than those that don't.[3] Yet a clear understanding of an organization's culture and values helps employees be more engaged, productive, and loyal, especially when the culture and values are in alignment. Developing and maintaining a strong culture and set of values requires ongoing effort, but it's worth it for the many benefits it can bring.

Empowering Leadership and Permission to Craft

In a study conducted in Norway among three hundred and thirty one workers, empowering leadership was found to be positively related to employees' permission to engage in job crafting strategies along three key dimensions: increasing structural job resources, increasing social job resources, and increasing challenging job demands.[4] The results suggest that empowering leadership is an important antecedent of job crafting. Employees who feel satisfied, motivated, and supported by their managers are more likely to be productive, engaged, and willing to job craft. A happy and healthy workplace is good for business, and there are a number of things employers can do to foster these conditions. But creating a positive work environment starts with effective and empowering leadership.

Frederick Herzberg's (controversial) motivation-hygiene theory, published in 1966, posits that there are two types of factors that affect motivation: hygiene factors and motivators.[5] Hygiene factors are those that, if absent, will cause dissatisfaction, but their presence will not necessarily lead to satisfaction. Examples of hygiene factors are working conditions, salary, and company policies. Motivators are those factors that, if present, will cause satisfaction, but their absence will not necessarily lead to dissatisfaction. Examples of motivators are recognition, responsibility, and opportunity for advancement.

Herzberg's theory is important in understanding job crafting because it highlights the roles of both motivation and satisfaction in the workplace. According to Herzberg, if we want to be motivated at work, both motivators and hygiene factors should be present. However, job crafting allows us to take control of our own motivation by creating a job that fits our needs and goals. In other words, we can use job crafting to create our own motivators, rather than relying on the presence or absence of hygiene factors. When we craft our jobs to fit our needs and goals, we are more likely to be satisfied with our work because we are motivated by the things that are important to us rather than by the things that are simply required of us. As a result, job crafting can lead to increased satisfaction and motivation in the workplace.

Henley Business School research has found major ways that managers and employees can help ensure satisfaction with work.[6] First, managers need to be clear about expectations and provide employees with the resources and support they need to do their jobs well. As leaders set high but realistic expectations, they make allowances for their staff members to learn from their mistakes as they strive for excellence. They also create opportunities for employees to share their ideas and feedback. Second, leaders can, through constructive feedback of employee performance, raise their employees' self-confidence, which boosts morale. Within this kind of positive nurturing context, heightened self-efficacy and greater awareness of competence is often an outcome that is associated with employees' self-initiated role adjustments on the job.[7] Third, leaders can encourage job crafting by raising employees' identification with the organization. Employees with a stronger identification with the organization are more likely to look beyond their self-interests and job craft in ways that benefit the organization.[8] Leaders can achieve this by communicating their organization's goals and priorities with a view to encouraging employees to buy-into these goals. Where employees adopt the organization's goals as theirs, such cognitive perception may be used to legitimize crafting behaviors.[9] Finally, it's essential to provide employees with opportunities for professional development so they can feel challenged and motivated in their roles.

By investing in your employees, you're investing in your business. When all these factors come together, you create a workplace that is enjoyable to be a part of and where employees are more likely to thrive. And that's good for everyone involved.

Personal Values and Permission to Craft

Employees' personal values are what they believe to be important in their lives and what guides their behavior. Values are what they use to make decisions if they find themselves in a difficult situation. Personal values can be different from other people's values, and they can also evolve over time, so that what is considered a value at the moment may not be important later on. It is important to encourage employees to think about their personal values to ensure that they are living a life that is true to who they are. Some examples of personal values include honesty, loyalty, compassion, family relations, friend care, love, freedom, justice, knowledge, and success.

In applying this to yourself as an individual, it may be useful to begin with asking: What are some of your personal values? Think about what is important to you and why it is important to you. Write down your thoughts so that you can refer back to them later. It can be helpful to think about your personal values when you are making decisions in your life. If you are unsure about what to do, you can ask yourself if the decision is in line with your values. For example, if you value honesty, you would not want to lie about where you were last night. If you value family connections, you might choose to spend more time with your family even if it means giving up some of your free time. Your personal values are an important part of who you are. They shape how you see the world and how you make choices. When you know your values, you can live a life that is authentic to you. One of the most important things you can do in life is to live your authentic self. This means being true to who you are, and not living a false version of yourself. It can be difficult to be authentic, especially if you feel like you have to conform to certain standards or expectations. But it's important to stay true to yourself because only then will you be truly happy and fulfilled. If you're not sure how to start living your authentic self, here are some tips:

1. *Be honest with yourself.* Take some time to think about who you really are and what you want out of life. Be honest about your desires, your fears, and your goals.

2. *Don't compare yourself to others.* It's easy to get caught up in comparing ourselves to others, but it's important to remember that we are all unique individuals. Focus on your own journey and don't worry about what anyone else is doing.

3. *Be true to your values.* What are the things that are most important to you? Make sure that you're living in a way that aligns with your values.

4. *Follow your heart.* Trust your intuition and listen to what your heart is telling you. This is the best way to stay true to yourself.

5. *Take risks.* Don't be afraid to step out of your comfort zone and try new things. It's the only way you'll grow and learn more about yourself.

Living your authentic self is important for a happy and fulfilling life. Start making changes today, and you'll be amazed at how much better you feel!

The first step in the job crafting framework is to understand the permission structures that exist in your organization. Once they are understood, individuals can start to craft their job to fit their own needs and goals. If you are not sure what the permission structures are in your organization, start by asking your manager or HR representative. They should be able to tell you what is explicitly allowed and what the organization's values are. If you still are not sure, observe the behavior of other employees and look for patterns. Do people generally take initiative and try new things, or do they stick to the status quo? Do people who take risks and push boundaries get rewarded or punished? The answers to these questions will give you a good idea of the organization's implicit permission structures.

Once you understand the permission structures in your organization, you can start to craft your job to fit your own needs and goals. If you are allowed to take initiative and try new things, you can start to think about how you can change your job to make it more interesting and challenging. If you are not allowed to take risks, you can still craft your job to fit your needs by finding ways to work within the existing rules and norms. That said, we recognize that risk taking can difficult, especially if you have hitherto lived a relatively safe and predictable life. But taking more risks can lead to richer and more fulfilling life experiences. Here are a few tips on how to take more risks in life:

1. *Get out of your comfort zone.* This is probably the most important step in taking more risks. If you're comfortable with your current situation, it can be hard to push yourself to try new things. But getting out of your comfort zone is essential to taking more risks. You'll never know what you're capable of unless you challenge yourself.

2. *Be prepared for failure.* When you take more risks, there's always the chance that you'll fail. But that's okay! Failure is part of life; it's part of how we learn and grow. If you're prepared for the possibility of failure, it won't be as devastating when it does happen.

3. *Trust your gut.* Sometimes the best way to know whether you should take a risk is to listen to your gut instinct. If something feels right, go for it!

4. *Know your limits.* It's important to know when to stop taking risks. There's no need to put yourself in danger just for the sake of being daring. Be smart about the risks you take.

5. *Have fun!* Taking risks should be enjoyable, so make sure you're doing something you actually enjoy. Life is too short to do things you don't want to do.

Taking more risks can be scary, but it's also exciting and full of potential. So go out and seize the day! You might surprise yourself with what you're capable of. If you're the type of person who doesn't like to take risks, you can still find ways to make your job work for you. There are always ways to work within the existing rules and norms, and by doing so, you can still get what you need and want out of your career. Of course, it's not always easy to play it safe. And there are times when taking risks is the only way to get ahead. But if you're careful and thoughtful about your choices, you can minimize the chances of failure and maximize your chances of success. So if you're looking to craft a career that fits your needs and lifestyle, don't be afraid to think outside the box. And remember, even if you don't take risks, there are still ways to make your job work for you.

Of course, no matter what type of organization you work in, there are always going to be some rules and regulations that you have to follow. However, by understanding the permission structures in your organization, you can start to craft your job in a way that fits your own needs and goals. Doing so demonstrates the critical links between granting the permission to craft and task, relational, and cognitive job crafting. When these are congruent it allows for a flow state to be achieved, which can increase job satisfaction and meaning.[10]

There are a number of practical ways in which permission to craft can be achieved. One way is to start with your values. What is important to you? What do you care about? Once you have identified your values, you can begin to look for ways to align your work with those values. For example, if one of your values is social justice, you might look for ways to volunteer with or donate to organizations that support social justice causes. Or, if you value creativity, you might look for ways to be more creative in your work, such as by starting a side project or pursuing a creative hobby. Another way to achieve permission to craft is to look at the organizational values of your company or organization. What does your company stand for? What are its goals? Again, once you have identified these values, you can begin to look for ways to align your work with them. For example, if one of your company's values is environmental sustainability, you might look for ways to reduce your environmental impact at work or to champion sustainable initiatives within your company. Ultimately, permission to craft comes down to finding ways to work within the existing rules and norms of your organization in a way that fits your own needs and goals. By doing so, you can create a job that is more satisfying and meaningful to you. As a result, you will be more likely to find lasting motivation and satisfaction in your work. It's no secret that everyone wants to find motivation and satisfaction in their lives. We all want to feel as though we're doing something that matters and that we're good at. Unfortunately, it's not always easy to find those things. The good news is that it is possible to find lasting motivation and satisfaction in your life. It might take some time and effort, but it is definitely achievable. Here are a few tips to help you get started:

1. *Figure out what you're passionate about.* One of the best ways to find lasting motivation and satisfaction in your life is to figure out what you're passionate about. What are the things that make you excited and eager to get started on? Once you know what your passions are, you can start working on pursuing them.

2. *Set goals for yourself.* Another great way to find lasting motivation and satisfaction in your life is to set goals for yourself. Having something to work toward can be a great motivator. Make sure your goals are realistic and achievable, though, so you don't get discouraged along the way.

3. *Find a role model.* One final tip for finding lasting motivation and satisfaction in your life is to find a role model. This could be someone who has already achieved what you're striving for or someone who embodies the qualities you want to possess. Seeing someone else achieve success can help you believe that it's possible for you too.

Case Study

The case concerns Rafael, the manager of Solera, a car dealership in Niterói, Brazil, and how he adopted job-crafting practices to navigate the constraints and crisis imposed by the pandemic on his organization. Rafael had been a manager at Solera for three years when the pandemic broke out. Prior to the pandemic, he had managed a team of twelve salespeople who were responsible for selling new and used cars at the dealership. When the pandemic started, Rafael was faced with the challenge of having to reduce his team's size by 50 percent owing to the decrease in demand for cars. He was also faced with the task of ensuring that the salespeople who remained on the team were productive and motivated, given the new circumstances. Rafael decided to take a proactive approach by crafting his and his team's jobs to better match the current context.

First, he gave his team members license to job craft. Solera was founded in 1990 by two friends, Ronaldo and José Antonio. They started by selling five cars out of Ronaldo's garage, and over time, the business grew significantly. They worked extremely hard on the business, hoping for a comfortable retirement. Thirty years after they sold their first car together, and as both Ronaldo and Jose Antonio were approaching seventy, Solera had a good share of the new and semi-new car market in Niterói. However, the company was facing inefficiency issues and stagnant growth because of inadequate structure. There was high turnover among employees, who often took customers with them when they switched agencies, along with low levels of standardization. This reinforced the partners' preference for centralizing decision-making.

Rafael's journey began just after he completed an MBA program at one of Rio's top business schools. With a young family, he opted for a job in an investment bank shortly after graduating. Even though he knew he would not last on the job, he did it to allay the economic concerns of his wife. Three years later, Rafael had lost all enthusiasm for his job, which was an integral aspect of his identity. His wife then encouraged him to leave his job because she wanted Rafael to be happy. The bonuses Rafael accumulated over three years would help keep the family afloat until he got a new job. Fortunately for Rafael, from a conversation at an informal gathering, the job at Solera came through a close friend who also happened to be Ronaldo's grandson. Rafael was asked to help Solera with constructing and moving the dealership to a new site.

Rafael took on the tasks of solving the challenges of the construction project and relocating Solera to the new site. He took full advantage of the total freedom he was given by Ronaldo and his partner, who were both tired of dealing with problems and surprises on the construction project. Rafael took charge and decided to turn the project into a sustainable building, which he had always been passionate about. He assembled a new building that no environmental activist could criticize. It included the use of solar panels, rainwater for washing cars, glass architecture for natural lighting, and other environmentally friendly initiatives. His building drew the attention of other car dealerships in the area, such that he began exploring the possibility of building a company offering his service and expanding into other markets.

While Rafael was figuring out his new business ideas, he was approached by Ronaldo and his partner to join the dealership as a manager to help them address the growth challenges they were facing. Though reluctant, he accepted the job partly because it offered a stable income and was also two blocks from his home, which would allow him take part in family activities that mattered to him. On accepting the job, he quickly realized that he did not have as much freedom as he thought he would have. He came up with some clever initiatives to drive sales and growth, all of which were rejected by the partners. Every creative move Rafael made was met with stiff opposition from the partners and subsequently dropped. In growing frustration, Rafael decided to put some of his knowledge from his MBA into practice. He began to focus on other aspects of the business he was interested in, such as formalizing processes, defining clearer roles for positions in the firm, and implementing a management system that ensured transparency of information on the purchase and sale of cars. He also began internal training and knowledge exchange avenues for employees, as well as engaging employees and partners with his new tool. He further invested in strengthening relationships with key stakeholders such as suppliers, banks, and finance companies, which resulted in greater benefits for customers who financed car purchases through Solera. He contacted other car dealers to buy their cars at below-market prices so that they could achieve their monthly sales goals, which built a win-win relationship. Beyond these initiatives, Rafael also explored starting a rental car division for the dealership.

It was at the height of his business adventures that the pandemic struck. Knowing difficult days were ahead, he approached the partners to structure a COVID-19 plan, which was again met with reluctance. The partners were not convinced the pandemic would affect their town and business. A few weeks later, the Brazilian government announced the closure of businesses and schools, and the whole economy ground to a halt. Back home with his family, Rafael felt he was once more in a familiar place where he was free to initiate ideas without any limitations. His first concern was his workers, who he knew had no savings. Rafael joined the government scheme that guaranteed they were all paid minimum wage as long as the lockdown lasted. For his salespeople, for whom the minimum wage represented a significant pay cut, he created further revenue-generating opportunities through his Facebook business, which emphasized sustainability. With the order closing physical businesses still in effect, Rafael's started looking for innovative ways to reach clients. He conducted surveys of existing customers, offering new exchanges and various options. This approach represented a significant departure from the traditional passive approach to sales. Even though there was a decrease in consumer spending, Rafael believed the crisis was driving the market, and clients could either seek liquidation of assets or fulfill their wishes of owning a dream car if their means permitted. He achieved outstanding results by arranging partnerships with other stakeholders, which created a win-win situation for all parties involved.

Eventually Rafael shared some results with Ronaldo, but without providing much detail regarding the changes he had implemented. Despite meeting the usual resistance, he found the talks useful for refining his ideas and envisioning new ways of solving different problems. He felt the need to receive some feedback about how the partners viewed his initiatives and was genuinely committed to doing his best, but he acted according to his own values.

As this case study demonstrates, the car dealership partners expected to hire a manager who would follow the job description to the letter and not attempt innovation. In other words, the manager was expected to continue doing what Ronaldo and his partner had done for many years while they built the business. Yet Rafael had also been hired to grow the company, which had stagnated, largely because of the traditional top-down approach to job design, complemented by a culture of excessively top-down control of employees. Even though the top-down approach seemed necessary because of the business's history of high employee turnover, it was the root cause of the dealership's failure to grow and was therefore counterproductive to the very purpose of employing Rafael. The outcome was the constant rejection of all Rafael's initiatives by the partners. What Rafael demonstrated, even within the constraints of his job, was the ability to craft his job to meet his own expectations of an innovative job that had employees and other stakeholders at its heart but would still achieve the overall goal of growing the business, which he did. This craving for meaningful work through impactful innovation made him leave his first job with the investment bank and subsequently informed his reluctance to take up managerial employment. Even though he practiced job crafting before the pandemic started, the pandemic allowed Rafael to gain further autonomy in his job, which created opportunities for him to use structural, relational, and cognitive job crafting to make changes to the car dealership.

If managers hold the reins too tightly, employees may feel they lack agency and meaning in their work and become disengaged. Employees can drive the solutions regarding their disengagement—but will managers give them the space to implement them? Given the compelling positive impact that making thoughtful changes to the design of a job can have on both employees and managers, we certainly hope so. Particularly now, when the job structure for individual contributors is rapidly changing, it will benefit both managers and employees to place greater emphasis and responsibility on individuals to master their destiny at work. Successful job crafting relies on explicit reciprocity between leaders and their employees at work, particularly with respect to negotiating the allocation of resources (time) between KPIs and other areas to focus on. The onus is on employees to demonstrate the impact of crafting on agreed KPIs, particularly if it requires tasks over and above the employee's regular role. Of course, employees can't deviate too far from their position, but this flexibility does provide them with the platform for building more extensive networks and gaining exposure to different thinking. We explore in greater depth each of the approaches mentioned in our four-step framework in the coming chapters.

In summary, job crafting is a win-win process—research consistently finds it positively impacts a host of outcomes beneficial to both workers and their organizations. These include increases in self-reported engagement, happiness, organizational commitment, job satisfaction, readiness to change, self-efficacy, and colleague-rated performance. Arguably the most relevant studies have found that job crafting enables workers to cope with stress, reduce exhaustion, improve well-being and resilience, and minimize the likelihood of burnout.[11] How? By using job crafting as a preventative mechanism, workers can redesign their jobs in a way that ensures they have sufficient motivational challenges (e.g., completion goals or increased responsibility) and supportive resources (e.g., autonomy, feedback, or colleague support) to cope with the demands of their jobs (e.g., interpersonal conflict or role ambiguity) without succumbing to stress and burnout.

In addition to helping workers manage their job resources and demands, and in turn their well-being, job crafting can be used to facilitate development. Tasks and relationships can be added to roles to broaden horizons and experience, and elements of the role can be reimagined to serve a different purpose. Crafting can also benefit those approaching retirement, enabling pre-retirement workers to decrease the job demands, which commonly cause individuals to want or need to retire.

5 Creating a Safe Climate for Job Crafting

The second element in the framework for job crafting given in chapter 1, namely, providing employees with a psychological safe space in which to craft, is taken up in this chapter. By creating an environment in which employees feel comfortable sharing innovative ideas, an organization creates opportunities for employees to experiment with new methods and potentially make mistakes without fear of judgment or scrutiny. To enhance the impact and implementation of employees' ideas, managers should ask the right questions of employees, such as "What are your strengths that the team can count on you for?" "What are some of your strengths that are currently underutilized by the team?" "What's a recent mistake that you made, but that you learned a lot from?" and "What skills or areas of improvement are you trying to develop?"

Climate versus Culture

It is important to understand the difference between an organization's climate and its culture. Culture is the deep strata of values, beliefs, and assumptions that guide behavior. Climate is the observable norms, behaviors, and energy in the organization. A widely recognized definition of climate sees it as

> a relatively enduring characteristic of an organization which distinguishes it from other organisations and (a) embodies members' collective perceptions about their organisation with respect to such dimensions as autonomy,

trust, cohesiveness, support, recognition, innovation and fairness; (b) [is] produced by member interaction; (c) serves as a basis for interpreting the situation; (d) reflects the prevalent norms and attitudes of the organisation's culture; and (e) acts as a source of influence for shaping behaviour.[1]

In other words, culture is made up of a collection of fundamental values and beliefs that give meaning to organizations. An organization's culture is often more implicit than its climate.[2] Organizational climate consists of more empirically accessible elements, such as behavioral and attitudinal characteristics.[3] Experts propose a further distinction, namely, that an organization's climate consists of shared perceptions whereas its culture consists of shared assumptions.[4]

Organizational culture develops over time and is influenced by the founders, leaders, and employees. It is represented by the things that are important to the organization and how that importance is expressed. For example, if innovation is valued, then employees might be encouraged to take risks and try new things. If employee satisfaction is a priority, then policies and practices might be in place to support that goal. An organization's climate is more changeable than its culture and is shaped by the day-to-day interactions between and among employees. It manifests in the emotional tone of the organization and in how people interact with one other. A positive climate is characterized by trust, respect, and cooperation. A negative climate might be characterized by fear, anxiety, and conflict. Leaders play a key role in creating and maintaining both culture and climate. By modeling desired behaviors and implementing policies and practices that support the organization's values, leaders can influence the culture. And by fostering a positive climate through their interactions with employees, leaders can create an environment that supports employee engagement and productivity. Organizational climate, therefore, is the prevailing atmosphere within an organization. It is the result of the organization's culture, values and norms, as well as the behaviors of its employees. Organizational climate can have a significant impact on employee morale, motivation, and productivity. For instance, research has consistently shown a strong positive relationship between organizational climate and corporate performance.[5] A positive organizational climate is often associated with high levels of employee engagement and satisfaction. A negative climate, on the other hand, can lead to increased absenteeism, turnover, and conflict.

Organizational climate is therefore an important factor to consider when managing an organization. When it comes to creating a positive organizational climate, there are a few key things that managers can do. First, it is important to clearly communicate the organization's vision and values to employees. Employees need to know what the organization stands for and what its goals are in order to be motivated to work toward them. Second, managers should create an environment that is conducive to open communication and collaboration. Employees should feel that they can openly share their ideas and opinions without fear of retribution. Finally, managers should focus on creating a positive culture within the organization. This can be done by encouraging employees to participate in company events, by recognizing and rewarding good performance, and by investing in employee development. Creating a positive organizational climate is not an easy task but is essential for any organization that wants to be successful. By taking the time to invest in their employees and create an environment that is conducive to open communication and collaboration, managers can ensure that their organization is one that attracts and retains the best talent.

Organizational Climate and Job Crafting

Creating a safe climate for Job crafting can be done in several ways. One way is to create an open and trusting relationship with employees. In managing teams, it's important to have an open and trusting relationship with individuals and team members. In such a relationship they will feel comfortable raising concerns or questions they may have and will be more likely to trust your decisions and follow the guidance of their team leaders. Research shows that trust is found in three qualities of workplace relationships. First, trust grows when members of the organization perceive each other and especially the leaders as credible or believable. That is, leaders are perceived as having integrity such that what they say can be believed, and beyond this, their actions align with their words. Trust also depends on how employees experience respect. This can be realized in the extent to which they feel included in decision-making, are supported through their professional growth, and receive care and attention on the job and outside the job. Finally, trust grows from the notion that one will be treated fairly by others so that regardless of position or status in the organization, equitable treatment can be expected.[6]

To build a relationship of trust, managers should start by being accessible and approachable. Make yourself available to answer questions and address concerns, and let your team know that you're open to feedback. Be sure to communicate openly and honestly with your employees. Let them know what you're thinking and feeling, and give them the opportunity to do the same. Finally, show that you trust and value their input by making decisions together whenever possible. By following these tips, you can create a relationship of trust and openness with your employees that will help make your team more successful. Workplace trust is essential for businesses to function effectively. Employees need to trust that their colleagues are competent and have good intentions. Managers need to trust that their employees will do their jobs well and follow company policies. Without trust, businesses would grind to a halt. Mistrust can lead to conflict, absenteeism, high turnover, and low productivity.

There are several things that businesses can do to foster trust in the workplace:

- *Clearly communicate expectations and objectives.* Employees need to know what is expected of them so that they can meet those expectations.
- *Encourage open communication.* Employees should feel comfortable communicating with their managers and colleagues.
- *Promote collaboration.* Working together toward a common goal can build trust.
- *Be transparent.* Share important information with employees so that they can make informed decisions.
- *Reward good performance.* Recognizing and rewarding employees who do their jobs well fosters trust.

Building trust in the workplace takes time and effort, but it is essential for businesses to function effectively. By taking steps to promote trust, businesses can create a positive work environment in which employees are productive and motivated. This will allow employees to feel comfortable discussing their work with you and brainstorming ways to improve their job crafting. Organizations today are under constant pressure to be more innovative and agile so as to compete more effectively in the marketplace. To meet this challenge, many companies are turning to workplace brainstorming as a way to generate new ideas and solve problems. Brainstorming has been shown to be an effective tool for stimulating creativity and promoting collaboration among team members. When done properly, it can help employees think outside the box and come up with creative solutions to challenges. To conduct a successful workplace brainstorming session, there are a few key things you should keep in mind:

1. *Create a safe environment.* Employees should feel comfortable sharing their ideas without fear of judgment or criticism. This climate of inclusivity has been shown to benefit individuals, teams, and organizations by enhancing individuals' feeling of self-worth, which also enhances their degree of engagement and commitment.

2. *Encourage wild ideas.* The goal is to generate as many ideas as possible, so don't worry about whether or not they are feasible at this stage. This is often the first rule of brainstorming. Allowing every possible idea to be put on the table before sifting through them.

3. *Build on each other's ideas.* Encourage employees to build on each other's ideas to create new and innovative solutions. Innovation builds on existing ideas, which helps avoid blind spots while fostering robust ideas.

4. *Keep it focused.* Make sure the session stays focused on the task at hand. If it starts to stray, gently bring it back to the topic at hand.

There are a few things leaders can do to make workplace brainstorming more effective. The first is to encourage participation from all employees. It is important to get input from as many employees as possible. Introverts should be encouraged to participate by asking them for their ideas in writing beforehand or breaking out into smaller groups. Second is the use of visual aids. Using visual aids can help stimulate creativity and help employees "see" the problem in a new way. Post-It notes are a great way to do this. Third is to set time limits. Setting time limits can help keep the session focused and on track. Try to keep each brainstorming session to no more than thirty minutes. Fourth is to ensure there is follow-up after the session. Once the session is over, leaders must be sure to follow up with employees on what was discussed and next steps. This will help ensure that ideas are actually implemented and not forgotten about.

Another way to create a safe climate for job crafting is to provide employees with the resources and support they need to be successful. This includes ensuring that employees have the tools and training they need to do their jobs effectively. It also means providing employees with opportunities to learn new skills and grow in their careers. By investing in employees, leaders can create a more productive and positive work environment for everyone. A learning organization is one that continuously adapts and improves in response to the changing needs of its employees, customers, and other stakeholders. In order to create a learning organization, leaders need to create an environment that encourages employees to share knowledge and be open to new ideas. Leaders also need to provide employees with opportunities to learn new skills and improve their existing ones. One way to encourage employees to share knowledge is to create a culture of openness and transparency. Employees should feel comfortable sharing their ideas and suggestions with others, and they should know that their input will be valued. Leaders can promote this type of culture by holding regular open forums where employees can share their thoughts and ideas. Another way to create a learning organization is to provide employees with opportunities to learn new skills and improve their existing ones. Leaders can do this by offering training and development programs that allow employees to gain new knowledge and skills. Additionally, leaders can create mentorship programs wherein more experienced employees guide and support less experienced ones.

Creating a learning organization requires leadership commitment, time, and resources. However, the benefits of doing so are numerous. A learning organization is more adaptive and responsive to change, it improves employee engagement and motivation, and it leads to better overall organizational performance. Thus, creating a learning organization is an important goal for any leader who wants his or her organization to be successful in the long term. Creating a learning culture within your organization can have a number of benefits. It can help attract and retain top talent, ensure that employees are staying abreast of changes in your industry, and boost morale and engagement. A learning culture doesn't happen overnight—it takes time and effort to build. But the payoff is worth it, both for your employees and for your business.

Building a learning culture starts with leadership. As a leader in your organization, you set the tone for how employees will view learning. If you see learning as something that's important and valuable, your employees will too. You can promote a learning culture in a number of ways, such as offering training and development opportunities, establishing mentorship programs, and encouraging a growth mindset among your employees. Doing so will help them see challenges as opportunities for learning and growth rather than as threats. It can also help them be more open to feedback and willing to take risks.

As a leader, you can set the tone for a learning culture by being a role model for lifelong learning yourself. Make sure you are staying up-to-date on developments in your industry, and encourage your employees to do the same. Pursuing continuing education opportunities, such as by taking courses or attending conferences, can show your employees that you value learning and that you're committed to staying at the forefront of your industry. By creating a learning culture within your organization, you will be setting yourself up for success in the long term. Your employees will be more engaged and motivated, better able to adapt to change, and more likely to stick around. And all of this will lead to better overall performance for your organization. If you're not already working on building a learning culture within your organization, now is the time to start.

Finally, you can create a safe climate for job crafting by making it part of your organization's culture. This means promoting and encourage employees to engage in job crafting. It also means supporting employees when they do engage in job crafting, and being open to hearing their suggestions. The best way to get employees to share their suggestions may vary depending on the organization, but one key is to create an environment where employees feel comfortable sharing their ideas. This can be done by ensuring that leadership is open to hearing employee suggestions and by encouraging employees to share feedback through regular communications and recognition programs. Additionally, it is important to ensure that employees understand how their suggestions will be used and that they will be kept informed of any changes that are made as a result of their input. By following these steps, organizations can create a culture of openness that will encourage employee engagement and improve bottom-line results.

Psychological safety is the belief that one can show up and be authentic without fear of negative consequences. It is a shared belief on a team that everyone is safe to take risks, experiment, and speak up with new ideas. Psychological safety has been shown to be a key driver of team performance. Google's Project Aristotle found that psychological safety was the number one predictor of team success.

Creating a psychologically safe environment starts with the leader setting the tone. Leaders need to model vulnerability by being open about their own mistakes and challenges. They also need to create structures and processes that encourage everyone to speak up. When teams experience psychological safety, they are more likely to take risks, experiment, and innovate. If you want to create a psychologically safe environment for your team, here are a few things you can do:

1. *Set the tone as a leader.* Be vulnerable and open about your own mistakes and challenges.
2. *Encourage everyone to speak up.* Create structures and processes that make it safe for people to share their ideas.
3. *Foster a culture of learning.* Help your team members learn from their mistakes and grow in their careers.

4. *Celebrate failure.* Encourage your team to take risks and experiment, even if it means failing sometimes.

Creating a psychologically safe environment is essential for any team that wants to perform at its best. By taking steps to encourage vulnerability and open communication, you as a manager can help your team members feel safe to take risks, experiment, and innovate. This will lead to better team performance and, ultimately, better business results.

6 Tools for Job Crafting

The third element in the framework for job crafting outlined in chapter 1, providing employees with the tools they need to job craft, includes the provision of enabling tools for task, relational, and cognitive job crafting. With task crafting, the focus is on finding ways to make our jobs more interesting and meaningful through changing what we do day-to-day. This might involve taking on new responsibilities, learning new skills, or simply approaching our work in a different way. Relational job crafting entails making changes to the social aspects of our jobs, such as modifying and enhancing our interactions with co-workers, supervisors, and clients. This could involve seeking out social support at work, taking on a mentorship role, or working to build better relationships with those we interact with on a daily basis. Cognitive job crafting involves making changes to the way we think about our jobs, such as reframing negative experiences in a more positive light or finding ways to see our work as contributing to a larger goal. This could involve setting personal goals, redefining our job roles, or simply changing our outlook on our day-to-day tasks. No matter what type of job crafting we undertake, the goal is always the same: to make our jobs more satisfying and enriching experiences. This chapter explores autonomy, control, trust, and decision latitude as key factors in job crafting.

Autonomy and Control

Autonomy, mastery, and purpose are three important factors that contribute to motivation. Daniel Pink in his book *Drive: The Surprising Truth about What Motivates Us* discusses how these three factors are essential for us to be motivated at work.[1] Autonomy denotes the state of being self-governing, of having control over our own lives and destinies. We need to feel that we are making our own choices and decisions rather than being controlled by others. Mastery denotes authority or the possession of a skill. We need to feel that we are good at what we do, which in the work context is associated with a feeling of making progress and achievement. Purpose refers to a goal or intention. We need to feel that our work is meaningful and has a positive impact on the world. Daniel Pink argues that if we want to be motivated at work, we need to have autonomy, mastery and purpose. Pink believes that these three factors are more important than money or other extrinsic rewards. *Drive* is based on research in the field of motivation and provides readers with a new understanding of what motivates us.

Autonomy is the capacity of an individual to make choices independently, without being subject to external constraints or influences. In its simplest form, autonomy can be described as self-rule or self-government. In the work context, autonomy manifests in the degree of control and discretion employees have over their activities. It implies empowerment to shape the work environment in ways that enable employees to perform to their best. Autonomous individuals have the ability to make decisions and take action without guidance or direction from others, even if that means going against the wishes of others. Autonomy also extends to groups and organizations. A group can be autonomous if it is able to function independently of outside control or interference. For instance, at the Gerson Lehrman Group's global headquarters in New York, employees don't have assigned team spaces but work in flexible working spaces called neighborhoods. Neighborhoods have key facilities such as meeting rooms, conference rooms, lockers, and so on. Workers are free to "pick up and relocate" to another neighborhood when they see fit. They also have highly autonomous workflows, especially the engineers. Engineers choose their own projects, engaging with business operators across the company directly—no project manager, no product manager.[2]

An organization can be autonomous if it has the power to make its own decisions and pursue its own goals without approval from a higher authority. The concept of autonomy has been important in philosophy and ethics since ancient times. In the Western tradition, it was first discussed by Aristotle in his *Nicomachean Ethics*. The idea resurfaced in the works of Immanuel Kant and John Stuart Mill. In recent years, autonomy has become an increasingly prominent topic in debates about morality and ethics. This situation owes in part to advances in technology, which have given individuals greater control over their own lives. As technology continues to evolve, the question of how much autonomy we should have is likely to remain a contested and controversial issue.

Nonetheless, evidence from different fields of study show that autonomy is a basic human need that, when satisfied, enhances civic behavior, has economic benefits, and boosts creativity as well as productivity.[3] The writings of the British economist Alfred Marshall and the philosopher John Stuart Mill provide some theoretical grounding to the arguments that work autonomy may enhance the likelihood of employees behaving according to their own values and goals, which in turn underpins the notion of integrity or the feeling of wholeness at work, where the feeling of being true to oneself gives employees the permission to be at their best at all times. Indeed, as self-determination theorists have shown, feeling internal assent regarding one's behavior, rather than feeling controlled or pressured, is strongly related to self-esteem and proves essential for well-being and effective performance in social settings.[4] In psychology, determination theory suggests that people are motivated to pursue their goals because they believe these goals are attainable.[5] This theory has been used to explain a wide variety of phenomena, including persistence in the face of failure and why people are more likely to achieve their goals if they have a strong belief in their ability to do so. A great deal of research supports the notion that belief in one's ability to reach one's goals plays a significant role in motivation. For example, numerous studies have found that when people believe they can succeed at a task, they are more likely to put forth the effort required to achieve it. In addition, beliefs about one's ability to reach a goal have been shown to affect how people respond to setbacks. Specifically, people who believe that they can succeed are more likely to persist in the face of failure and less likely to give up.[6] Determination theory has been used to explain a wide variety of phenomena, including educational attainment, job performance, and even voting behavior. In each of these areas, researchers have found that people who have a strong belief in their ability to reach their goals are more likely to be successful than those who do not.[7] This research provides strong support for the notion that determination plays a significant role in motivation and achievement.

As Mill wrote, this ability to self-govern, "like other faculties, tends to improve by practice, and becomes capable of a constantly wider sphere of practice."[8] In the work context and from a job-crafting perspective, this leads to a higher level of voluntary participation. Evidence suggests that across Europe, autonomy across all skills levels was been in continuous decline over the decades, yet the need to prioritize well-being in response to the effects of the pandemic may force organizations to rethink how they address autonomy and the key concerns associated with its absence. For instance, Lloyds Bank has an internal platform called Gigs. Gigs refers to short-term, side-of-desk projects and activities that are undertaken in addition to the day job, occupying no more than a few hours a week. Gigs are volunteering opportunities, and the platform itself is used to advertise projects and activities; colleagues with the requisite skills and knowledge can express interest in a gig. Gig activities are carried out in addition to their current business as usual responsibilities. The platform allows employees to job craft by finding opportunities within the organization to showcase their skills, work with other departments or divisions with which they may hitherto not have had any association, and, most important, feel fulfilled in the process. From the organization's perspective, it offers a cheaper way to get jobs done as different departments enlist the help of other departments on a project basis to execute tasks. The alternative would be to outsource these tasks to external stakeholders, which is typically expensive. Interestingly, all employees have the autonomy to choose what projects or listings they apply for based on the skills they have and in the process job craft across task, relational, and cognitive levels to enjoy their work better.[9] This example shows the importance of autonomy for personal growth and self-fulfillment at work. It also shows how a simple intervention such as launching this platform in a large organization supports worker autonomy, purpose, and mastery altogether for the benefit of all.

The absence of autonomy may result from excessive forms of control. The classic theories of motivation, coercive and excessive control stem from a "theory X" notion of motivation that suggests employees are inherently lazy, lacking in ambition, and not motivated to come to work, such that the only way to get something out of them is to adopt an authoritarian management style whereby managers closely monitor and supervise each employee. To address this, it must be made clear that allowing for autonomy does not imply relegating control into irrelevance. Hence it is crucial to note that autonomy does not in any way imply isolation. In other words, being autonomous does not mean working without collaborators or supervisors. Also, autonomy does not mean doing anything, anyhow, anywhere. Organizations with high levels of employee autonomy usually define the boundaries within with employees can exercise their decision-making power. They create an environment and set certain bounds within which employees can choose a degree of autonomy. Finally, autonomy does not mean working without a net. By this we mean interventions, guidance, mentoring, and established protocols. Autonomy must not be conflated with a lack of guidance or direction, which in all probability would result in a dysfunctional workplace. With this point clarified, the ideal autonomous context provides for a balance of control. In other words, both employees and employers have certain levels of control that allow both parties to agree and collaborate to achieve the goals of the organization. Underpinning this balance is a culture of openness and trust among stakeholders to cocreate meaningfully for the benefit of all.

Decision Latitude and Trust

Decision latitude is a term used in organizational psychology to describe the freedom an individual has to make decisions. The concept was first introduced by J. Richard Hackman and Greg R. Oldham in 1974 in their job characteristics model, which posits that decision latitude is one of five core job dimensions that affect employee motivation and satisfaction.[10] Decision latitude has been shown to be positively correlated with job satisfaction, and employees who have high levels of decision latitude are more likely to report higher levels of job satisfaction and engagement.[11] Additionally, research has shown that decision latitude is a predictor of job performance, meaning that employees who have more freedom to make decisions tend to perform better on the job.[12]

What does this mean for organizations? If organizations want to create a work environment that is conducive to employee motivation and satisfaction, it is important to ensure that employees have a high degree of decision latitude. They must have the freedom to make decisions about their work and the authority to do so—both of which are controlled by the organization. Additionally, if organizations want to improve job performance, they should focus on increasing employees' decision latitude.

There are a few different ways to do this, but one of the most effective is to give employees more control over their work. For example, employees could be allowed to set their own schedules, choose their own projects, or make decisions about how they complete their work. Organizations could also create teams that are responsible for making decisions about their work, rather than having a single leader who makes all the decisions. Whatever approach is taken, the goal should be to give employees more control over their work, and to create an environment in which they feel empowered to make decisions. By doing so, organizations will not only improve job satisfaction and performance, they will also create a more positive and productive work environment for everyone. For instance, on self-managing teams, each member is responsible for their own work and decisions. This type of team is often seen in startups and other fast-paced environments where decisions need to be made and implemented quickly. Self-managing teams can be very successful, but there are also some challenges that come along with this type of team structure. First, it can be difficult to establish clear roles and responsibilities for team members. Second, self-managing teams can sometimes become too leaderless, which can give rise to confusion and conflict. Finally, because each member is responsible for their own work, it can be difficult to hold members accountable if they are not meeting expectations. If forming a self-managing team on the basis of such higher degrees of decision attitude is under consideration, it is important to weigh the pros and cons carefully.

The first thing to do is to review the goals of the team in question and consider whether or not a self-managing structure would help achieve the set goals. Additionally, it is important to think about the dynamics of the team and whether or not the members would be able to work well together without clear roles and responsibilities. Finally, it is important to ensure there is a plan in place for holding members accountable so that the team can run smoothly.

With respect to designing workloads, there are a few things to keep in mind. First, consider what is to be achieved with the workload. Is the goal to try to increase productivity? Improve customer satisfaction? Reduce costs? Once the goal is clear, the next steps focus on designing a workload that will help the organization achieve the goal. Our research into this posits a few tips to help:[13]

1. *Set realistic workloads.* This is crucial for self-managing teams, or indeed in organizations wanting to implement higher levels of decision latitude. If workloads are too ambitious or unrealistic, employees are likely to feel overwhelmed and give up, yet if they are not ambitious enough, the right results won't emerge.

2. *Take into account your team's skills and experience.* Not everyone is able to handle the same workload. Tasks must be assigned based on individual team members' abilities.

3. *Be flexible.* Things will inevitably come up that were not planned for. Rather than getting frustrated, be prepared to adjust workloads as needed.

4. *Get feedback.* After a few weeks, check in with the team to see how it is doing. Ask for team members' perceptions of what's working and what isn't. Get their feedback, and make adjustments.

By following these tips, organizations can design workloads tailored to needs and goals. With a little bit of planning, productivity can be boosted and the needed results attained. Hence, improving decision latitude is a function of a two-way trust system that has also been proven to have positive effects on the organization as a whole. A *Harvard Business Review* article, "Let Employees Choose Where, When and How to Work," reports that companies that officially allow employees to choose to work remotely at least three times per month, for instance, are more likely to report revenue growth of 10 percent or more.[14] This suggests allowing employees the ability to choose their own remote working schedule within this boundary can only work well if all parties trust each other. The article proposes three ways organizations can work with employees to improve the decision latitude within the organization:

1. *Ask employees* what kind of freedom they want, and be willing to act on their indications.

2. *Deepen understanding* of remote working tools.

3. *Be more vocal* about policies relating to freedom.

These three actions highlight the fact that trust is essential. Several research articles posit that trust is the basis of quality interpersonal relationships and a source of competitive advantage for organizations.[15] Trust is important not just in vertical relationships, that is, between employees and the organization's leadership, but also in horizontal relationships with fellow co-workers. Co-workers are usually colleagues within the organization who have relatively equal levels of power and authority and with whom employees interact more frequently during workdays. Trusting co-workers entails being willing to be vulnerable to the actions of fellow co-workers whose behavior and actions one cannot control. Hence, when employees are asked to describe the kind of freedom they want, the organization must be willing to act on these prescriptions to give employees latitude on issues they consider most important to them. Similarly, deepening the understanding of remote working and remote working is crucial to making decision latitude work better. The media organization NationSwell requires employees to work together in a central office on Mondays, but they are free to work from coffee shops or wherever they choose the rest of the week.[16] This type of decision latitude could also apply to choosing when during the day to accomplish tasks so that employees can synchronize tasks with their chronobiology for maximum effectiveness. Also, several organizations are known to have fully distributed teams. Mozilla, Upworthy, StackExchange, and GitHub, to name a few, are known for having fully or largely distributed teams, which they often use to their advantage to recruit talent from all over the world, wherever the candidates may live. And since conversations around four-day workweeks and other remote working accommodations have come to the fore during and after the pandemic, demystifying this aspect of work is crucial for organizations to create trust regarding the decision latitude afforded employees.

Yet allowing higher levels of autonomy and decision latitude in organizations as tools for facilitating job crafting often faces some key resistance. As discussed earlier, the challenge of maintaining adequate levels of control while allowing workers increased autonomy remains a critical issue. The next section explores this challenge.

Balancing Autonomy, Decision Latitude, and Control

The ideals of autonomy and higher degrees of decision latitude in the work environment, though appealing, come with significant issues and constraints. Managers are often concerned that crafting provides employees with an excuse to drop their primary tasks and responsibilities, not realizing that crafting, if done well, aligns with employees' strengths, motives, and values. Managers can allow employees discretion in designing day-to-day work and task activities intended to fulfill work goals; the key is striking a balance between alignment and autonomy (or empowerment) and control so that managers become enablers rather than enforcers. We found that managers who remove impediments rather than create them through bureaucratic practices can ensure employees do not misuse job crafting to drop their tasks and responsibilities but rather use it as a means to enhance the achievement of their daily work goals.

While autonomy manifests in the degree of freedom and independence individuals or teams within an organization may have, alignment denotes the extent to which individuals and teams share a common purpose by working toward the same goal. A crucial point to note is that autonomy and goal alignment are not mutually exclusive. Organizations often see the relationship between autonomy and goal alignment as a competition between two ideals such that more autonomy means sacrificing focus and organizational alignment, while more alignment means less autonomy and increased command and control. This view sees both alignment and autonomy as two ends of a spectrum in which the more an organization tilts toward one end, the less of the other they get. However, this is not the case; the two are not mutually exclusive. As Stephen Bungay writes in *The Art of Action,* this conflict is a misconception.[17] The two ideals are not in competition with each other but should exist in harmony. In fact, what research and practice seem to suggest is that alignment through transparency or trust, as discussed earlier, enables increased autonomy. When seen this way, the relationship is shown in a 2×2 matrix in figure 6.1.

The two lower quadrants illustrate what happens when low alignment is joined to low or high degrees of autonomy. Where there is very limited coordination on common goals and purpose and there is low autonomy, the result is high levels of micromanagement and indifference. Such organizations can be quite static and monotonous. Joining high autonomy to low alignment, on the other hand, results in an entrepreneurial but chaotic organization. The freedom to pursue different agendas could prove beneficial but could also ultimately be problematic as the ensuing chaos might be detrimental. The upper

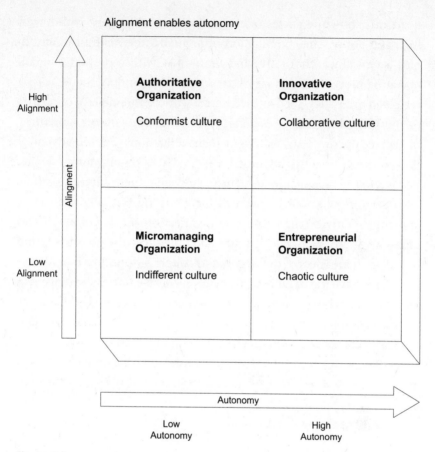

Figure 6.1

Alignment enables autonomy, as conceived by Henrik Kniberg, from "Is Kniberg's Aligned Autonomy Matrix Still Relevant?," Org Topologies, May 26, 2023, https://www.orgtopologies.com/post/is-kniberg-s-aligned-autonomy-matrix-still-relevant#:~:text=For%20Kniberg%2C%20autonomy%20is%20linked.

quadrants show the effects of combining high alignment with low or high autonomy. The combination of high alignment with low autonomy is typically authoritative and conformist, with very strict standard operating procedures and very little room for autonomy. Some heavily regulated industries, such as the pharmaceutical and medical industries or the finance industry, may call for high alignment-low autonomy by default owing to the nature of their obligations. Yet the advent of fintech shows how this alignment can coexist with autonomy—which takes us to the final quadrant, namely, high alignment-high autonomy. Organizations that fall within this quadrant are typically innovative and collaborative. This is the goal or direction organizations should aspire to attain such that through alignment, goals, objectives, and boundaries are clearly defined but through autonomy, individuals and teams have the latitude to innovatively decide how those objectives are met. This is how innovation on teams can be harnessed. The leader's job is to communicate what problem needs to be solved and why, and the teams collaborate with each other to find the best solution.

Studies of organizations that have found high levels of alignment and autonomy show there are at least three ways this can be achieved:

Hire the "Right" and "Best" Hands

Hiring is a top priority when trying to create a high alignment-high autonomy culture. Organizations that have done so well tend to hire around three C's—character, chemistry, and competence. To build an organization of high alignment and autonomy, it is not sufficient to hire for competence alone but also for character and chemistry. Having people with the right character and the right disposition to fit into the culture of the organization ensures they can be both self-directed and collaborative as necessary. Hiring people who are very competent but unable to work well with others could prove detrimental to the entire organization's direction. A former Spotify executive describes recruits of this sort as "talented jerks." The company's recruitment exercises focused on filtering out candidates who were too self-centered and not team-aware. This was achieved by scrutinizing how candidates described their previous work: did they talk about themselves or about other people? The best way to predict future behavior is to evaluate past behavior.

Manage Process and People Well

Depending on the stage of development of an organization, high levels of alignment and autonomy could easily be achieved by different means. For mini-startups, which tend to be very flat and collaborative, alignment and autonomy are baked in. However, as such firms grow, it becomes pertinent to manage alignment better. Automattic is an organization known for making WordPress. It currently has over two hundred employees. It began the active process of managing alignment once it had fifty people on its teams. The firm set up a system of having team leads who allocated work and provided direction. This helped keep teams aligned with key priorities and collaborating with other teams as necessary in the delivery of objectives. Decision-making occurs in mixed fashion all the way from the top (providing general strategic direction) through team leads (providing mainly prioritization, coordination if there is team crossover, and helping teams focus) to the team, which often decides how duties will be allocated and executed. In other words, top-down communication helps provide direction and purpose—the "why"—and small teams decide how to go about finding the best solution—and it's the team leads who largely make sure everyone's in alignment.[18] The job of managers in high autonomy-high alignment cultures is to help people see and make progress and to ensure clarity on what progress entails. This is achieved by providing guidance and support at all times.

Promote Social Accountability and Transparency

Progress at all levels in the organization requires a lot of transparency, information distribution, and social accountability. For instance, projects and daily milestones should be communicated to all teams clearly to help everyone stay on the same page and hold themselves and others accountable for the progress required to happen. Organizations like the game developer Supercell use daily key performance indicators to guide all employees beyond just the executives. At Automattic, transparency is a key value of the organization; the team uses the tool iDoneThis to keep abreast of tasks that have been accomplished and the progress still required. Along with other forms of internal communication organized by various teams, this helps create better alignment between teams such that rather than information being siloed, decisions and discussions are documented, shared, searchable, and viewable by everyone in the company. When knowledge is decentralized and accessible to everyone, decisions can be made quicker and people can own their tasks. This also means power is distributed and knowledge sharing helps align the teams on the organization's goals.

The United Kingdom Oil and Gas Sector: A Case Study

The UK's oil and gas sector is at the nexus of difficult twenty-first-century issues. Automation is fundamentally reshaping the industry, with routine physical and data-handling jobs at high risk of obsolescence. The sector was badly hit by the pandemic, with mounting job losses as investment was delayed or canceled. Perhaps most fundamentally, the oil and gas industry is itself declining as the UK shifts from its traditional dependence on fossil fuels toward cleaner energy sources. Organizations have to adapt to such sea changes by adjusting their business and people strategies to align with the future energy sector and the postpandemic global economy. For employers, this complex blend of challenges makes the goal of improving employee experience even harder to achieve.

The Need for an Individual Perspective
Aiming for a multiskilled and versatile workforce that can help the UK energy sector reach net zero carbon emissions, the oil and gas industry's core strategy is to retrain and reskill the existing workforce while

also attracting new recruits possessing the skills needed by the future workplace.[19] The future looks—tentatively—bright: research by Robert Gordon University in Aberdeen, Scotland, indicates that a high proportion of skills are transferable between traditional fossil fuels and lower-carbon energy sectors, and there is already much collaboration between employers, industry bodies, and government bodies aimed at bridging the gaps.[20]

But research by Kirsty Denyer at the Henley Business School in Reading, England, highlights that the oil and gas workforce is made up of individuals with unique lives, careers, and ambitions.[21] Some individuals will be proactive in moving to the clean energy sector. Others won't wave good-bye so easily to their professional identities and will want to leverage their years of experience by continuing their existing oil and gas careers. Considering the oil and gas workforce as a single entity, to be reallocated to the burgeoning clean energy sector as required, makes too many assumptions. The challenge for employers in this perfect storm, then, is to keep the focus on the individual worker and create an environment in which employees can retain control of their career paths and ways of working: there is no one size fits all solution. That is easier said than done for organizations already tackling multiple complex strategic issues.

Flexible Working in Oil and Gas: The Dark Side

The oil and gas industry has a unique relationship with flexible working. It has long been characterized by periods of boom and bust, with semiregular cycles of hiring and firing when oil prices plummet or rocket up (though the impact of the pandemic, followed by dips in oil prices between 2022 and 2023, was unprecedented). That is, flexibility has long characterized the oil and gas industry—often to the benefit of employers and at the cost of stability and security of employees, many of whom are highly skilled knowledge workers.

Denyer's research indicates that this is a tough environment for employees, who are beset by anxiety and the uncertainty of living contract to contract, or the perennial risk of waking up to a tax form every

Monday morning. An individual needs a suite of ready resources when the axe does fall: a financial cushion to tide one over, social support from friends and family, professional networks to draw on, and the ability to quickly identify and highlight transferable skills and tailor their presentation to fit any jobs that may come up. Psychologically, adaptability and resilience are necessary qualities for such truly flexible working—something many oil and gas workers in the physically demanding offshore environment have. Working in the oil and gas industry may be an extreme example of working flexibly, but it is also a reminder to be careful what you wish for when you wish for greater job flexibility.

Dr. Selin Kudret, an associate professor in leadership at the Henley Business School, explains what hybrid work is, points out the enablers and derailers of remote work, and offers a model of "remote leadership" so that hybrid work can be leveraged for the long-term benefits it provides for both businesses and employees.[22] Seismic shifts have occurred in the workplace, with hybrid work gaining traction. According to Kudret, the pandemic only accelerated a trend that had been gaining pace with advances in technological tools enabling remote and asynchronous work. She identifies four main types of flexible work: remote work (i.e., work conducted remotely, out of office or out of the workplace), flextime work (i.e., work conducted outside the traditional nine-to-five workday), reduced-hours work (e.g., part-time work), and compressed-hours work (e.g., the contractual hours are completed across four days rather than five). Hybrid work is a type of flexible work characterized by flexibility as to both the place and time of work. With the pandemic having mandated physical separation to control the spread of the virus, hybrid work began to indicate place flexibility and remote working. From research evidence dating back to before the pandemic, we know that flexible work is associated with a raft of desirable outcomes for employees, businesses, and the society, such as improved employee productivity and performance, a reduced gender pay gap, a more diverse talent pipeline in the workforce and at leadership and board levels, greater agility in responding to fluctuating market demands, and improved health and well-being for employees and their family members, all of which bring about intangible benefits and tangible results for stakeholders, says Kudret.

Why has flexible work become highly contentious now despite the positive evidence from the prepandemic world? Kudret offers a number of explanations. Flexible work, such as remote work and flextime work arrangements, had been offered as an employee benefit by some employers before the pandemic. For instance, according to the CIPD (Chartered Institute of Personnel and Development) 2019 UK Working Lives Survey, the majority (61 percent) of respondents reported remote work was not available in their organizations.[23] The same study reported that for 53 percent of respondents, flextime was not possible either. As such, during prepandemic times, both the availability and actual take-up of flexible working arrangements had been fairly limited. Then, almost overnight, the pandemic enforced in particular remote working arrangements: according to data released by the UK Office of National Statistics, almost half of the working population ended up working remotely during the first lockdown (April 2020).[24] This massive shift caught organizations, individuals, and society unprepared. Therefore, the time in which remote working was at its peak coincided with a rushed, distorted remote work experience. Many firms did not have adequate technological tools to enable remote work at the time; there was a lack of individual choice (volition) over the degree of remote work; social support mechanisms, such as childcare, were not available at all; and leaders mostly lacked the skills to lead from a distance. These conditions were not the best in which to test an otherwise versatile work arrangement. This first brush with a distorted version of remote work became a crucial source of the current controversy over the effectiveness of remote work, Kudret suggests. Moreover, what was once offered as an employment benefit has since become commonplace, a silver lining of the pandemic, and that places extra pressure on employers to keep up with the Joneses in the workforce market. Now, two years after the pandemic, some of these conditions have changed for the better. That should help us experience a better version of remote work. Most businesses are in a better place to provide technological tools that facilitate remote work and team collaboration. Social support and childcare options have been becoming increasingly available. Working fully from home has increasingly evolved into a hybrid arrangement combining remote work and in-person work.

According to Kudret, despite these enabling conditions, there are still major challenges that help or hinder hybrid work arrangements in reaching their full potential in the postpandemic world. Developing remote leadership capabilities is one of the key determinants of the success of hybrid work and will also help organizations shape a culture that doesn't stigmatize remote work. Remote work necessitates a shift toward a remote leadership mindset, which Kudret describes as knowing how to lead people from a distance in a way that allows leaders to get back to their own tasks and relationships. In leading remote work, leaders need to assume the role of an agile broker weighing goals, tasks, and resources, says Kudret. This means a heavier focus than before on leaders' task competence and planning. Leaders will not be able to play it by ear as employees are no longer present in the same physical and time sphere. Keeping the team focused on goals and their delivery and spotting and responding to emerging needs for resources should be among the key task behaviors of leaders. Kudret anticipates that work will need to be organized more in terms of tasks and outputs and less according to the traditional person-hour system. The unit of compensation will accordingly shift from time units to output units as institutional control of employees' working space and time becomes obsolete. Kudret also argues that, in leading remote work, leaders need to gear their relationship behaviors toward addressing people's basic innate psychological needs—autonomy, relatedness, and competence. Leaders should carefully choose the influence tactics that will communicate recognition of employees' technical knowledge and their desire to strengthen relational ties with the organization. Influence tactics, such as rational persuasion, consultation, and inspirational appeal, must replace hard tactics such as controlling and legitimating. The psychological need for autonomy manifests as volition in hybrid work. In the context of hybrid work, volition is the personal choice of the degree of remote versus office-based work, continues Kudret. Leaders must respect individual choice as employees may assign different degrees of importance to a particular work mode at different stages of their working lives. To gain commitment and collaboration from employees, leaders should facilitate both remote and in-person work depending on an employee's personal choice, as opposed to enforcing a certain percentage for each— and mandating a full return to in-person work is a surefire way to crush autonomy and spark a backlash, Kudret concludes.

Practicalities and Implications

This chapter has posited that employees should be allowed to revise their work identity and meaning through job crafting, which in turn would be expected to influence their attitudes and motivation for the better. As such, job crafting can improve career commitment, which makes work more meaningful. Several tools are available to achieve this goal. Job autonomy provides employees with freedom, discretion, and independence to proactively craft their jobs according to their personal preferences, needs, and abilities.[25] Job crafting as a self-initiated action enhances motivation and self-determination.[26] Research demonstrates that job autonomy may often lead to greater commitment, personal growth, greater job satisfaction, and improved well-being. According to theories of self-determination, job autonomy motivates employee job crafting, which facilitates a better fit between individuals' preferences and needs and their jobs. Individuals' self-determined motivation may be met by proactively changing their job tasks and work roles to help fulfill personal needs.[27] Job autonomy provides employees with the choice of adjusting the cognitive, relational, task, and physical aspects of jobs to satisfy needs and preferences. These self-initiated behaviors decrease the misfit between personal preferences and creates a safer work environment for employees, which in turn rewards organization in the form of employees who have a stronger sense of calling and ultimately greater commitment to their jobs. When organizations provide the right tools for crafting, the outcome is employees with greater commitment, often accompanied by a passion for and dedication to professional self-actualization[28]. Job autonomy therefore provides employees with better control, which enhances commitment.

Job autonomy provided by organizations allows employees to flexibly arrange their schedules and methods to complete their jobs. To support employee preferences and needs, organizations need to be aware of individual differences in managing job design. Managers may encourage employees to temporarily or permanently change the tasks of their jobs. By encouraging relational job-crafting behaviors, for example, managers can motivate employees to build their own support networks among colleagues within the organization as a way to feel more supported in the workplace. Also, actively finding different channels of communication within the organization can facilitate information sharing and better alignment on goals so that tasks are completed more efficiently. Regarding cognitive crafting, managers can encourage and actively engage employees in transforming their daily routines into clearer career missions, which should buttress a stronger sense of calling and purpose. For employees, having meaningful work may facilitate positive perceptions and behaviors at work. To ignite a personal sense of calling toward current jobs, organizations may start by mapping a clear and long-lasting vision and mission, developing authentic leadership, and nurturing respectful social interaction to emphasize the significance of committed relationships. This chapter suggests that these tools help job crafting have the desired effects in organizations, thereby creating a win-win situation for all stakeholders.

7 Capacity to Job Craft

This chapter explores how managers can create capacity for job crafting along the three dimensions introduced in chapter 1—task, relational, and cognitive crafting—through ensuring realistic workloads, clear role boundaries, and protected time to job craft, for example by allocating time for innovative thinking. It also explores how organizations can further create capacity and signal their commitment to job crafting by altering reward systems to recognize employees who demonstrate out-of-the-box thinking and by providing opportunities for employees to learn new skills and acquire knowledge through job-related training and development programs. While these efforts may meet operational or cultural challenges, they enable employers and employees to develop task, relational, and cognitive landscapes that bring meaning to work.

Realistic Workloads

The role of a realistic workload in enabling job crafting was explored briefly in the previous chapter in relation to leveraging decision latitude as a tool for job crafting. The purpose of setting realistic workloads is to provide room for team members and their leaders to reflect on and engage in the process of job crafting. The notion of a realistic workload must align with both the organization's and the individual's perspective. That is, both individuals and the organization must agree on what a realistic workload looks like. Agreement can only be attained by crafting a careful balance between job demands and job resources, a process that involves all stakeholders in actively deciding on and designing work requirements.

According to job demand–resources theory, job demands are "those physical, psychological, social, or organizational aspects of the job that require sustained physical and/or psychological (cognitive and emotional) effort or skills and are therefore associated with certain physiological and/or psychological costs."[1] Workloads are often seen as a component of job demand, implying that certain aspects of work entail costs and consistent effort. Job demand can be high in very demanding roles, or low in repetitive and less taxing roles. Because of its potential to enhance employee well-being through the creation of positive work environments, research has often suggested that job crafting is more likely to occur in enriched environments. Enriched environments are work environments full of resources (i.e., co-worker social support, task variety, autonomy) and challenging demands (a challenging workload, emotional demands, technology demands). Work environments that are unenriched have the tendency to create state boredom as job demands and resources are very low. Bored individuals in an unenriched work environment are less likely to job craft.[2] In other words, job demands and job resources both influence task job crafting, while emotional demands are often related to cognitive and relational job crafting, implying different paths between demands and resources and various job crafting activities. The search for realistic workloads is therefore a search for workloads that are challenging and exciting enough to encourage crafting but not so stressful as to lead to burnout. Job demands consume energy and require a lot of individual effort, which often places higher demands on energy resources.[3] By contrast, the availability of job resources activates a motivational process that allows employees to enjoy meaningful work by engaging in tasks, duties, and roles within the organization. Unless there is alignment of job resources and a person's needs, preferences, job demands, and abilities, workers will strive to level this issue by stabilizing demands and resources in their work environment through diverse job crafting activities. It need not be a reactive process; it could be proactively driven by organizations that value their employees.

From an organizational point of view, therefore, it becomes crucial to understand that job demand, often assumed to precipitate negative outcomes, can instead lead to positive outcomes through job-crafting activities. This implies that individual job crafting, a bottom-up process, may be as important as the traditional, top-down form of job design in the modern firm. In practice, as teams and individuals are assigned demanding tasks, allowing individuals to reflect on their aspirations, for instance, and on how the assigned tasks align or misalign with those aspirations fosters healthy, realistic workload management. Hotel staff members with an aspiration to become hotel managers someday might engage in different tasks with different departments as a necessary part of the process for realizing their ultimate dream; this would be an example of both relational and task crafting. Similarly, hotel staff members assigned to clean an entire floor of guest rooms may choose not to see it as hard work but as part of making travelers' journeys more comfortable, a form of cognitive crafting. It all comes down to how workloads are managed to create realistic setups that ensure both the organization and the individual feel the individual is sufficiently engaged within key parameters that forestall burnout.

Role Boundaries

Traditionally, role boundaries are defined by clear job descriptions. Through job descriptions employees know their obligations and the organization's expectations of persons in that role. A role boundary is a clear definition of the duties, rights, and limitations of employees within the work environment. Where organizations create the opportunity for employees to participate in the co-creation of these boundaries, job crafting is the inevitable outcome. With task crafting, employees are encouraged to shape or mold their roles by actively adding to or dropping the responsibilities set out in their official job description. For instance, a bus driver might choose not simply to convey passengers from one point to another but to serve as a tour guide by offering sightseeing advice to interested persons along the route. In such cases the task boundaries are adjusted to accommodate activities above and beyond what is expected of an individual in a given role. Yet task crafting must not be a messy process; it can and should be undertaken in a way that maintains clarity of expectations. Clarity around role tasks becomes particularly important in large organizations, where management of human resources may place more demands on leaders. In this type of organization, clear guidance can be provided on the parameters within which crafting is permissible, and crafting can be led by designated stakeholders within the organization, such as team leaders.

Based on the three key dimensions of job crafting, building capacity for job crafting while simultaneously maintaining clear role boundaries can be achieved through the following:

1. *Adjusting functional role boundaries* (e.g., crafting more decision-making latitude for developing oneself).
2. *Adjusting social role boundaries* (e.g., crafting support from colleagues).
3. *Adjusting mental role boundaries* (e.g., crafting more tasks or responsibilities, crafting fewer cognitive or emotional demands).

With respect to adjusting functional role boundaries, greater decision latitude can enable individuals to work with their team leaders to agree to adjusted functions, thereby making their jobs more personalized while embracing a wider range of tasks. Adjusting social role boundaries may include allowing employees to work with colleagues beyond their immediate departments for improved cross-functional collaboration. With respect to adjusting mental role boundaries, individuals can be empowered to take on more responsibilities within their own perceived capabilities. Across these dimensions, the critical issue is how to create equal access to job crafting for all employees to ensure they know the opportunities available to them to job craft. For instance, employees in more senior roles may cite limited time to engage in job crafting while more junior employees may cite limited autonomy as a major impediment to job crafting. While research has shown that individual personalities play a significant role in determining the propensity to engage in job crafting, the establishment of role boundaries where job crafting is to be entertained should at most be semirigid. In other words, even though there are set boundaries, they should provide only minimum expectations of individuals in their jobs. For a university professor, for instance, the minimum expectation is to teach, conduct research, and engage in citizenship activities. The specific nature of the citizenship activities or research undertaken is decided on largely by the individual according to the individual's own interests and aspirations. Engaging in policy dialogues and other matters of public significance, though not included in the professor's job description, may be a discretionary activity driven by interest—or it may be interdicted by the organization. Freedom may be provided for individuals to go above and beyond minimum expectations to job craft with clear purpose and intent and with the support of team leaders, but there may also be clear boundaries to what the individual is allowed to do.

Time to Job Craft

Solitude and dedicated time for reflection are not common in the modern organizational environment. Yet, as a best practice for enabling capacity to job craft, individuals in organizations can be allotted time to engage in job crafting. There are different ways of achieving this within the organization, as follows:

1. *Analyze current task obligations.* Invite employees to map out their current job obligations to explore the dominant activities that their current jobs entail. The reasoning behind this is to establish patterns on the job and together with the individuals constructively decide where changes can be made to bring about a more fulfilling job. This will then entail creating time for individuals to reflect on their passions, capabilities, and motivations while seeing how their current task obligations can be better aligned with these.

2. *Offer job-crafting workshops.* Job-crafting workshops allow more collective engagement in the process of job crafting. Workshops of this nature tend to begin with clearly communicated objectives around which activities are designed for group engagement. Researchers from the University of Michigan designed a typical two-hour job-crafting workshop and suggested that the workshop would entail drawing before and after sketches of attendees' jobs. The before sketch helps individuals take a step back and gauge how time and energy are spent at work. The after diagram helps individuals identify opportunities to craft a more ideal but still realistic version of their jobs. A job-crafting workshop often ends with a clear action plan, which will typically be run by team leaders to strengthen legitimacy.

3. *Hold job-crafting swap meets.* Swap meets are another innovative way to encourage and build active capacity for job crafting in organizations. Swap meets are gatherings at which enthusiasts trade or exchange items of common interest, typically items they can no longer use. One quick way of developing roles to suit employees while ensuring all tasks are assigned for someone to complete is to hold a swap meet. The idea is that employees trade assigned tasks to make their job lists more favorable. It is like a task trade by barter such that individuals are free to swap tasks with others and to pick up new tasks in the process. In the end, all required tasks will have someone assigned to complete them.

Research has shown that creating room for solitude and reflection on jobs has a strong positive effect on the overall well-being and performance of employees. A study of the effects of on solitude in leadership showed that solitude helps leaders focus on inner directionality toward growing authentic individual awareness as a moral person and a moral manager and promotes integration of inner and outer directionality toward ethical leadership, resulting in decision-making processes that will have an impact on others' perceptions of leaders' authentic ethical leadership. This study's finding is significant for job crafting because when time is created for innovative thinking and job crafting to happen in a safe space, individuals find an inner balance that makes work more meaningful to them, benefiting them and the organization.

Reward Systems

The time-tested carrot-and-stick approach is a good way to motivate individuals in organizations and to encourage certain types of behaviors. Where reward systems are designed to identity and reward individuals who have proactively engaged in innovative thinking, the likely outcome is that more people within the organization will be encouraged to do the same. However, this outcome might not be as straightforward as it seems because of the complex relationship of creativity to intrinsic or extrinsic motivation.

Recent research has highlighted the significance of employee creativity in enabling organizational effectiveness and innovation.[4] Therefore, a challenge managers of modern organizations face is to create the conditions necessary for creativity to flourish.[5] Several scholars have argued that high intrinsic motivation—that is, engagement in an activity for the internal rewards it brings the individual—is a necessary condition for creative achievement.[6] Likewise, many studies have shown that individuals who are intrinsically motivated are more likely to display high levels of creativity. In light of these viewpoints and findings, managers and organizations interested in boosting creativity should consider implementing practices and procedures designed to enhance employees' intrinsic motivation levels. For instance, managers might provide employees with opportunities to obtain intrinsic rewards by assigning them to jobs that are challenging and stimulating in nature. This type of reward, whereby individuals receive assignments with higher job demands, might be considered more beneficial insofar as the individuals are already intrinsically motivated.

Although research suggests that providing employees with intrinsic rewards has the potential to enhance creativity, the default position of many managers is to use monetary and other extrinsic rewards to stimulate creativity. Unfortunately, there is no consensus on the effects of extrinsic rewards on the creativity of employees. Studies have found that in some instances, offering extrinsic rewards boosts creativity and performance, while others suggest that this approach actually diminishes creativity by undermining the individual's intrinsic motivation. There is evidence in the literature to support both these positions.

The implication of these findings for managers desiring to build capacity for job crafting is that the challenge and complexity of jobs contribute in important ways to employees' intrinsic motivation and creativity. Specifically, complex jobs, those characterized by high levels of autonomy, skill variety, identity, significance, and feedback, are expected to encourage higher levels of intrinsic motivation and creativity than jobs that are relatively simple and routine in nature.[7] When jobs are complex, individuals are likely to be excited and enthusiastic about their work activities and interested in performing them for the sake of the activities themselves, conditions conducive to creativity at work. By contrast, extrinsic rewards were effective for enhancing creativity in employees doing simpler jobs. Hence rewards should be considered on the basis of level of difficulty of the individual's job and of ensuring appropriate reward mechanisms are associated with creative efforts in order to have an overall positive effect.[8]

Training and Development

Another way of enhancing capacity to job craft is to create opportunities for employees to learn new skills and acquire new knowledge through job-related training and development programs. Exposure to new skills programs provides a strong impetus for employees to job craft as they put their new skills to use. Where employees are encouraged to be proactive in their pursuit of new skills that in turn will build their career competencies, the effects on job crafting and subsequent engagement and well-being of the employees are usually very marked.

Research suggests that career competencies concern the acquired career-related knowledge, skills, and abilities aimed at achieving certain career goals. In an integrative theoretical framework on career-related competences, three major career competency dimensions were highlighted; the authors emphasized that organizations wanting to encourage job crafting via this means should examine them more closely. The first dimension comprises reflective career competencies, which concern the degree of awareness of, and personal reflections on, the career. For instance, individuals may reflect on their strengths and limitations, but also on their motivation and passion concerning their career. The second dimension comprises communicative career competencies, which focus on individuals' effective deployment of professional networks to communicate and demonstrate strength to others. An example of this competency is knowing whom to approach for a career advancement conversation, and how. The third dimension comprises behavioral career competencies, which entail setting goals and exploring career opportunities and learning. An example is the pursuit of further education to become a specialist in a work-related area.[9] In each of these three areas of career competencies, the direct implications for propensity to job craft are evident.

In line with our argument that a proactive personality is likely to be related to greater job crafting, research shows that a proactive personality is an important antecedent of job crafting. Because employees with a proactive personality are generally inclined to take initiative independent of the specific context, individuals with a proactive personality are also more likely to engage in job crafting behaviors, such as seeking job resources and challenges. Furthermore, research also shows that employees who crafted their job resources reported an increase in these resources over time.[10] These findings indicate that through job crafting, employees can change their job characteristics.

The National Health Service in the UK has in recent years encouraged capacity for job crafting through training and development. Owing to the shortage of nurses in the health service, different innovative means are being deployed to build nursing care availability. One of the proposed approaches is to offer interprofessional training. By this, other health care professionals cross-train to take on some new responsibilities in addition to their current roles in what can be described as enabling job crafting by different medical professionals. For instance, health care professionals who would typically not have any nursing-related task could take on some basic nursing duties as part of their daily tasks. In this way, some of the gaps in care created by the nursing shortage are being addressed in ways that allow other professionals in the system to engage in active training and development, all of which amounts to job crafting.

8 Conclusion

The world is going through rapid changes. Several macro variables influence how organizations design work that affects how employees see themselves in their jobs. More than ever before, well-being, purpose, and meaningful work are top priorities for employees and employers, well outside the traditional priorities of compensation and other extrinsic rewards. With this shift in focus comes the need to bolster employee engagement, which has been declining in recent years. The first and second chapters of this book presented job crafting as a way to solve the meaningful work conundrum many employers and their employees now face. It explored the why, what, and how of job crafting. First, why job crafting? Changes in the current global work landscape call for more innovative ways of addressing the challenges that come with them. While job crafting is not necessarily a new concept, it offers a significantly different approach to job design from most traditional organizational approaches. Global workforce mobility, the interdependence of industries, and the battle for talent, among other crucial factors, challenge organizations to do better if they want to retain their top talent. The rise of the gig economy and side hustles, which allow employees to earn more money for themselves and, most important, do what they are passionate about, threatens to dilute their commitment and engagement levels to 9-to-5 jobs.[1] Hence it is particularly beneficial for managers and leaders of organizations to help their employees find meaning in and connect with work. This may require that managers adopt strategies to craft their jobs in a way that allows them to respond to emerging challenges in the workplace. Not only do managers benefit from finding meaning in their work, they must also create conditions for developing an engaged workforce. What drives job crafting is the search for meaning in work with respect to what is done, with whom, and why, so that organizational outcomes are still achieved. As a modern take on job design, job crafting exemplifies empowerment directed toward designing meaningful engagement with work and in the workplace.

Next, what is job crafting? Simply put, job crafting is the proactive and intentional altering of one's job demands and resources to better align with one's own goals, strengths, and weaknesses. For managers, it is the practice of empowering employees to design meaningful work. The end result is always to make work more satisfying and engaging for the employee. Job crafting is a proactive, often unsupervised, modern take on job redesign that empowers workers to transform the jobs they have into the jobs they want by becoming design agents instead of passive recipients of job titles, responsibilities, and roles. The central premise is that workers can stay in the same position but get more meaning out of their jobs simply by changing aspects of what they do, interacting differently with others, and changing how they think about their work. This invites conceptualizing different dimensions to crafting: crafting what is done (task crafting), crafting work interactions (relational crafting), and crafting how work is conceived (cognitive crafting)..

In task crafting, employees and their leaders agree on changing the scope and boundaries of the employee's work. It involves making changes to task content, process, and outcome expectations of a job. In practice, it implies that employees and their leaders codesign or cocreate jobs that transcend the named duties of their job description but fall within the strength profile of the employee, thereby allowing her to get more out of her role. It is a reconceptualization of work that allows more meaning to be added to employees' existing work. This reconceptualization reframes the mindset, particularly how the employee perceives meaning and purpose in work. In contemporary organizations, task crafting is a must. With various technologies being deployed at work, especially the different artificial intelligence (AI) technologies that are adopted to facilitate work processes, the nature of managerial work is rapidly shifting. If the task of the manager is planning, scheduling, monitoring, maintaining control, and so on, it is now obsolete as AI applications easily perform these tasks and can issue forecasts for better management. As a result, managers are already placed in situations requiring task crafting even if they prefer the status quo. It is no longer a question of whether the manager must task craft. It is a question of how to task craft. As such, process innovation becomes crucial in crafting tasks into more meaningful and impactful roles. We proposed a two-step process to achieve this. The first step is decomposing each task into its constituent parts. This allows you as a manager to have a broad understanding of what your tasks actually involve. The second step is to examine the work processes that each task fits into or leads to. This entails stepping back to take a panoramic view of how your tasks fit into your bigger assignment as manager. Task sequencing offers visual clarity as to what comes first and what makes logical sense. In the process, you may observe gaps in your work, in which case you can take steps to fill the gaps or to eliminate redundancies.

Task sequencing leads to cognitive crafting, which requires us to reflect on how we think about and perceive work. The absence of meaning in work reduces a job to mechanical tasks that are unconnected to a wider purpose. This disconnect is often found as one of the dysfunctionalities of the classic bureaucratic organizational structure, where groups and teams operate within silos that do not share information or goals, or even talk to each other. The mental framing of our work is more powerful than we could imagine. The need for cognitive crafting comes from the observation that while doing daily routines, we are in a frame of mind that affects how we see the routine This explains why cognitive crafting is often described as a challenging dimension of job crafting: we must hold in mind an image of the redefined or recrafted work. In other words, the crux of cognitive crafting is to cognitively allocate resources to the outputs assigned to your primary job function and be willing to take on additional projects that provide different rewards. Cognitive crafting could occur where a person identifies with the organizational purpose. In teams where managers create a positive work culture and an atmosphere in which all employees are valued irrespective of their role, it is easy to have organizational members who redefine the purpose of their work and identity. When the floor cleaner of allegory at NASA uttered the storied phrase, "I am helping put a man on the Moon,"[2] it illuminated a way of thinking that cognitively crafted daily routine not as a menial job (which it fundamentally was) but as part of a bigger vision and effort. That is, cleaning as a job is part of the processes needed by the space mission. That was a brilliant piece of cognitive crafting on the part of the cleaner that reflected a profound sense of meaning and engagement at work.

With task crafting and cognitive crafting comes yet another dimension of crafting—relational crafting. People are an integral part of any work experience and often affect the extent to which employees are engaged with or disengaged from work. The popular HR saying, "People don't leave jobs, they leave managers," captures the vital importance of relational crafting in organizations. Like task crafting, relational crafting is an intentional approach to redefining the broad limits around whom an individual relates with in the workplace and how. By reprioritizing relationships in the workplace, relational crafting aims to create a meaningful balance for the manager between work aims and objectives, on the one hand, and, on the other, personal goals, needs, and values, available time, and value offered to others. In face-to-face contexts, relational crafting can be expressed through both formal and informal engagements such as work meetings, informal lunches, or discussions over coffee. Having some latitude to decide whom someone can work with on a job often brings immense satisfaction. Especially where jobs have been siloed, as happens in some large organizations and bureaucracies, having the opportunity to exit that silo and connect with other employees on projects and tasks is what relational crafting is about. It focuses on changing the relational boundaries of work along at least two distinct dimensions—the quality and quantity of interactions with others at work. Either way, the focus remains on achieving

the organization's objectives, but employees can adopt a more intentional approach to work relationships such that those goals are met. Yet
developing work relationships often comes with unintended consequences inasmuch as the role of technology cannot be ignored. The
mere fact that changes have occurred in relational boundaries at work
does not guarantee that trustworthy and healthy relationships will follow. Building empathetic, authentic, and trustworthy relationships at
work remains a key need that relational crafting also amplifies. We suggested three ways of addressing these relational needs:

- *Foster social connection.* This argues the need to intentionally craft
  relationships through meaningful and genuine social interactions.
  This can be achieved through formal as well as informal means
  (e.g., informal gatherings). Where crafting is based on supportive
  relationships, it stands a greater chance of doing well.

- *Prevent exclusion through meaningful participation.* This is accomplished
  through encouraging employees to participate in specific collaborative events in order to prevent situations where in-groups and out-
  groups can form. It also involves being deliberate in how activities
  are planned to ensure inclusivity is at their core.

- *Lead with transparency.* This involves designing policies that make
  clear how leadership takes place. It also means giving your employees, for instance, the right to choose what and how their personal
  data will be used by the company. To lead with transparency is to be
  as open as possible in aligning your actions with the organization's
  espoused values.

Yet with these benefits comes the bigger question, how? How can or
should job crafting be implemented in organizations? Chapter 1 con-
cluded by presenting some thoughts on how job crafting can be implemented in organizations as follows: provide employees with a *license* to
craft, provide employees with a *psychological safe space* to craft, provide
employees with the *tools* they need to craft, and provide employees
with sufficient *freedom* to craft. Each of these elements was explored in
greater detail.

Chapters 3 and 4 explored readiness for job crafting and providing the enabling permission to craft, respectively. In chapter 3 we posited that for job crafting to work well, both individuals and organizations must be ready for it. The key aspects of both organizational and individual readiness for job crafting explored in this chapter included culture, process, people factors, and some bottom-up approaches. Job crafting works in contexts that enable or facilitate it happening. An individual can make personal decisions to job craft cognitively, relationally, or taskwise. However, these dimensions of job crafting operate within the boundaries of what the organization allows. Where organizations remain flexible enough to accommodate job crafting, individuals can take the initiative to job craft. One way organizations demonstrate readiness for job crafting is by demonstrating malleability and openness in their processes. Processes help translate inputs into desired outputs or outcomes. Where processes have hard boundaries such that the content is unknown to employees, it makes the organization's processes resemble a black box—rigid, mysterious, unknowable. However, some processes have more porous boundaries. In such cases the organization is more welcoming of inputs from others so that the content diagram can be made smaller or bigger. For instance, the pandemic revealed that a lack of flexibility in organizational work processes or the unwillingness of managers to proactively render their work processes malleable made workers continue to appear in person for work when their work could, through job crafting, have been done remotely. Once the pandemic happened, many organizations were forced to innovate their processes.

A second aspect by which to gauge the readiness of both individuals and organizations for crafting is how well leadership creates an enabling environment for crafting. Leaders play important roles in contributing to workers' sense of meaninglessness, such as when employees feel their leaders take them for granted or when they are assigned work they consider meaningless. Where leaders are people-centric—that is, where they truly value people and desire to see them grow—a likely outcome is a free environment in which employees feel empowered.

The challenge is that in reality, different organizations and different industries may need different types of leadership. A people-centric leadership approach may be inappropriate in top-down leadership systems. However, our point in chapter 4 is that while a unidirectional leadership approach is easily attainable but unlikely to contribute to creating a safe space for job crafting to happen, organizations and leaders should consider omnidirectional leadership. Omnidirectionality is people-centric and accepts the fact that you as manager are also influenced by your colleagues, your employees, your stakeholders, and your customers. The French philosopher and anthropologist Bruno Latour would argue, even more radically, that you are influenced by your electronic devices, software, and other artifacts in your work environment in one way or another. This is because all these devices also participate in organizational life. Hence leadership that creates the atmosphere for job crafting must be relational in nature. In a postpandemic era in which work is largely intermediated by collaborative technologies, it makes sense to ensure that leadership is people-centric.

From an individual perspective, however, we think that the starting point to gauge readiness for job crafting is the recognition by the individual that there is a need—a lack of alignment between what an individual does and the individual's skills, desires and purpose—and that this need should be addressed. Awareness is key and helps bridge the gap between ignorance and knowledge. Where this gap is not bridged by an open acknowledgment, research shows that employees' typical responses to feeling a lack of purpose range from working to rule to operating in silos to total disengagement. Where such individuals are proactive, willing to communicate and discuss the situation with their leaders, crafting can be encouraged. This, however, speaks to a more personal issue of individual values through which individuals can assess meaning at work. We submitted that to be able to job craft successfully, an individual (whether manager or subordinate) should have clear personal values to act as an anchor for giving meaning to what they do, a strong sense of identity, which allows them to define fulfillment in more personal terms, and a support group that reinforces their identity and celebrates their achievements and successes. Beyond these, chapter 3 also discussed opportunities for job crafting. Such opportunities could arise from organizational growth or expansion, which broadens the scope of work beyond contractual terms. In such instances, as new acquisitions or expansions take place, structural adjustments typically follow, providing some room for changes to existing roles and boundaries. This is one good point where job crafting can happen. Other opportunities also arise where gaps are observed in organizations requiring innovative solutions to make necessary changes to tasks and relationships. Other particular challenges could also trigger job crafting by individuals, but chapter 3 posited that job crafting can be enabled and strengthened by creating enabling contexts and by having collaborative and positive relationships with colleagues.

Chapter 4 explored permission to craft. As in chapter 3, we delved into this topic from both organizational and individual perspectives. From an organizational perspective, organizational culture, structure, and values can function as facilitators of both implicit and explicit permission to job craft. Explicit permission structures are those that are written down and communicated to employees, such as in an employee handbook or a job description. Implicit permission structures are those that are not written down but are understood by employees from the organization's culture and values. Whereas culture in its simplistic form means how things are done around here, specific permission frameworks are created for job crafting. Where culture is more open and supportive of innovation, creativity, and flexibility, this may constitute permission to job craft since the artifacts of the organization, its values, and the underlying assumption openly support this type of activity. Beyond this, organizational culture has an impact on whether or not individuals have the flexibility to initiate tasks, projects, and relationships, and whether these changes are recognized and rewarded. Related to culture is the structure of an organization, which also has an impact on the ease with which individuals are able to engage in job crafting.

Organizational structure describes the arrangement of relations between the different parts and members of an organization. Formal organizational structures show the network of formal relationships and obligations in the organization. There are also more informal structures such as social structures. Both kinds of permission structure exist in organizations, so employees must understand them since they provide either implicit or explicit permission to job craft. Leaders and managers who see individuals making attempts are encouraged to lend their support by helping them navigate the implicit and explicit permission structures of the organization. Individuals who understand these structures can leverage their personal values to make decisions along the way. In most contemporary organizations, permission to engage in job crafting may not be written in black and white, but individuals and leaders must leave space for calculated risks in contemplating taking the plunge. It will involve getting out of one's comfort zone, being prepared for failure, trusting one's gut, knowing one's limits, and having fun in the process. Even where the context's allowance for crafting is not understood, some effort can be made in the direction of job crafting with the help of leaders and managers.

Chapters 5 and 6 discussed in detail how safe environments can be created in organizations for job crafting and the tools needed to do so. These two chapters explored the practical nuances of enabling job crafting in organizations. Chapter 5 discussed the importance of distinguishing between organizational climate and culture. Culture is widely understood to be made up of a collection of fundamental values and belief systems that give meaning to organizations and is often more implicit than organizational climate. Organizational climate consists of more empirically accessible elements such as behavioral and attitudinal characteristics. Leaders play important roles in influencing both culture and climate, which can have a significant impact on employee morale, motivation, and productivity. Hence building a positive climate helps boost the confidence of employees. A few ways of doing so include investing in employee development, fostering open communication, and creating opportunities for employees to have input into decisions that affect them. The end goal of building a positive climate is to develop trust between the key internal stakeholders of the organization. We posited that organizations can test how well a trusting environment is being built by asking three questions:

1. *How well do we communicate?*   This ensures that objectives and goals are clearly communicated and understood while also allowing for freedom of expression and communication from employees to leaders. Good communication also enables transparency, which is crucial to building trust. The emphasis must be on the qualitative aspects of communication, not just the quantitative aspects.

2. *How well do we collaborate?*   A good marker of trust is collaboration. Even though the structural requirements of organizations necessitate teamwork, the question is how well collaboration happens among teams and within the entire organization. It begins with ensuring that the environment is safe for collaboration, wild ideas are welcomed, ideas from others are built on, and sessions are focused.

3. *How well do we reward?*   What is valued is rewarded. Where trust is to be engendered in an organization, the use of rewards to ensure those who are deserving are rewarded also helps build trust.

Another way to create a safe climate for job crafting is to provide employees with the resources and support they need to be successful. This includes ensuring that employees have the tools and training they need to do their jobs effectively. Building a learning culture starts with leadership. As a leader of your organization, you set the tone for how employees will view learning. If you see learning as something that's important and valuable, your employees will too. As a positive work climate builds trust, leaders and managers can begin to make job crafting a part of the organization's culture. This means promoting and encourage employees to engage in job crafting.

Where the climate for job crafting is right, the conversation should shift to the question, what kind of tools might be needed for job crafting. In chapter 6 we explored some of the crucial tools for job crafting, namely, autonomy, control, decision latitude, and trust. Autonomy is needed for crafting to occur. The desire for autonomy is a basic human need that, when satisfied, enhances civic behavior, has economic benefits for the organization, and boosts creativity and productivity. The ability to self-govern, like other faculties, tends to improve with practice and becomes capable of an ever-increasing sphere of practice. Where organizations exercise stringent control, this feeling of autonomy gives way. While in practice, arguments could be made for stringent control in certain industries and types of organizations, care must be taken not to mistake "stringent" control for "stifling" control. With stringent control, boundaries are set within which autonomy is practiced, and those boundaries can be reviewed over time. There is still control but perhaps a very healthy form of control necessary to avoid Thomas Hobbes's state of nature ("the war of all against all"). Control and autonomy have been linked to motivation, resulting in calls for organizations to genuinely evaluate the extent to which employees have autonomy and the level of control the organization has, and the effects of these on employee motivation.

Similarly, decision latitude is a term used in organizational psychology to describe the freedom an individual has to make decisions. If organizations want to create a work environment that is conducive to employee motivation and satisfaction, it is important to ensure that employees have high levels of decision latitude. This means giving them the freedom to make decisions about their work and ensuring that they have the authority to do so. Building such self-managing teams with high levels of decision latitude can be achieved by setting realistic workloads, taking into account a team's experience and skills, being flexible, and getting feedback. Organizations can also actively enable decision latitude by doing the following:

1. *Asking employees* what kind of freedom they want, and being willing to act on their suggestions.
2. *Deepening their understanding* of remote working tools.
3. *Being vocal* about policies related to freedom.

Hence, when employees are asked to describe the kind of freedom they want, the organization must be willing to act on these revelations to give employees latitude on issues they consider to be most significant to them. Achieving this outcome requires trust. Trust emerges not just in vertical relationships, between employees and the organization's leadership, but also in horizontal relationships, with fellow co-workers. The challenge of increasing decision latitude in practice can be addressed by ensuring alignment of the individual's goals and the organization's goals. Whereas autonomy refers to the degree of freedom and independence individuals or teams have within an organization, alignment refers to individuals and teams sharing a common purpose as they push toward the same goal. The ultimate goal is to build an organization that operates with both high alignment and high autonomy. Organizations that achieve this state are typically innovative and collaborative. There are goals or directions an organization should aspire to attain such that through alignment, goals, objectives, and boundaries are clearly defined, but through autonomy, individuals and teams have the latitude to innovatively decide how those objectives are met. This is how innovation in teams can be harnessed.

Chapter 7 explored the capacity to job craft. Where the need for job crafting has been firmly established and thought given to how to begin, more practical steps follow in building capacity for job crafting. Chapter 7 posits that this process begins with realistic workloads. With respect to creating capacity to job craft, the purpose of setting realistic workloads is to provide room for team members and leaders to reflect on and actively engage in the process of job crafting. From an organizational point of view, therefore, it is important to understand that job demands, which are often assumed to cause negative outcomes, can yield positive outcomes through job crafting activities. In practice, as teams and individuals are assigned demanding tasks, allowing individuals to reflect on their aspirations and how the assigned tasks align or misalign with those aspirations fosters healthy and realistic workload management. Also, understanding role boundaries helps ensure capacity for job crafting is built. Where organizations create the opportunity for employees to participate in the co-creation of these boundaries, job crafting is the inevitable outcome. We proposed that working from the key dimensions of job crafting, building capacity for job crafting with a view to attaining clear role boundaries can be achieved through the following:

1. *Adjusting functional role boundaries* (e.g., crafting more decision-making latitude for developing oneself).
2. *Adjusting social role boundaries* (e.g., crafting support from colleagues).
3. *Adjusting mental role boundaries* (e.g., crafting more tasks or responsibilities, crafting fewer cognitive or emotional demands).

Creating time to job craft is also necessary. Solitude and dedicated time for reflection are not commonly available in the modern organization. Yet, as a best practice for building capacity for job crafting, individuals in organizations should be given time to actually engage in job crafting. This can be achieved by analyzing current task obligations, offering job crafting workshops, or holding job crafting swap meets. Creating space for solitude and reflection on jobs has a strong positive effect on the overall well-being and performance of employees. Job crafting can also be facilitated by orienting reward systems around job crafting and by making available training and development opportunities. When reward systems are designed to identity and reward individuals who have proactively engaged in innovative thinking, more people within the organization will likely be encouraged to do the same. Training and development opportunities have been shown to enable job crafting by providing the means for employees to learn new skills and acquire new knowledge related to their jobs. The acquisition of new skills is a strong impetus for employees to job craft so that they can put their new skills to use.

We strongly encourage leaders to become more deliberate in creating systems and climes that enable job crafting. As the labor market becomes increasingly tough and high rates of disengagement and well-being-related issues become increasingly topical, we offered in this book job crafting as a viable solution to building organizations that truly value their people as the core of their business. The insights shared provide a blueprint to start having conversations and to take the right steps in the right direction.

Notes

Preface

1. Gallup, *State of Global Workplace 2013*, October, 2013, https://news.gallup.com/poll/165269/worldwide-employees-engaged-work.aspx.

2. Juno.com, *The 2021–22 Workplace Culture Study*, October 2022, https://www.withjuno.com/download-workplace-culture-study.

3. Juno.com, *The 2021–22 Workplace Culture Study*.

4. Juno.com, *The 2021–22 Workplace Culture Study*.

5. University and College Union, *Workload Survey Data Report 2021*, June 2022.

6. Surtees, "What Do Employees Really Want from Their Workplace?"

7. Greg Iacurci, "The Job Market's 'Game of Musical Chairs' May Be Slowing—but Workers Still Have Power, Say Economists," CNBC, October 2022, https://www.cnbc.com/2022/10/04/the-job-market-is-cooling-but-workers-still-have-power-say-economists.html.

8. Unum, "Employee Benefits and Flexible Working Lead the Way in the War for Talent," November 2021, https://www.unum.co.uk/about-us/media/benefits-and-flexible-working-war-for-talent.

9. Instant Offices, "Lack of Flexibility Is a Deal-Breaker for More Than Half of Employees Worldwide," July 2021, https://www.instantoffices.com/blog/instant-offices-news/lack-of-remote-working-a-deal-breaker.

10. Ernst and Young Global, "More Than Half of Employees Globally Would Quit Their Jobs If Not Provided Post-Pandemic Flexibility, EY Survey Finds," May 2021, https://www.ey.com/en_gl/news/2021/05/more-than-half-of-employees-globally-would-quit-their-jobs-if-not-provided-post-pandemic-flexibility-ey-survey-finds.

11. Craig Powers, "SAPinsider Benchmark Report: The State of Human Experience in the Workplace," June 2021, https://workforcesoftware.com/press-release/workforce-software-partners-with-sapinsider-ibm-and-eightfold-ai.

12. HiBob, "Return to Work Study: Flexibility Drives Employee Happiness," May 2021, https://www.hibob.com/research/hybrid-work-drives-employee-happiness.

13. Juno, *The 2021–22 Workplace Culture Study*, October, 2022.

14. Oracle and HR Research Institute, "The State of Human Experience in the Workplace 2022," February 2022, https://www.oracle.com/a/ocom/docs/state-of-human-experience-in-the-workplace.pdf.

15. Terence Mauri, review of *The 3D Leader: Take Your Leadership to the Next Dimension*, interview by Ben Laker, September 20, 2022; see also Ben Laker, "The Benefits and Challenges of Remote Leadership in 2023," *Forbes*, January 19, 2023, https://www.forbes.com/sites/benjaminlaker/2023/01/19/the-benefits-and-challenges-of-remote-leadership-in-2023.

16. Ben Laker, Charmi Patel, Pawan Budhwar, and Ashish Malik, "How Job Crafting Can Make Work More Satisfying," *Sloan Management Review* (September 17, 2020), https://sloanreview.mit.edu/article/how-job-crafting-can-make-work-more-satisfying.

Chapter 1

1. Fangfang Zhang, Sabreen Kaur, and Sharon K. Parker, "Job Crafting," Oxford Research Encyclopedias: Psychology, September 15, 2022, accessed August 8, 2023, https://oxfordre.com/psychology/view/10.1093/acrefore/9780190236557.001.0001/acrefore-9780190236557-e-832.

2. William A. Kahn, "Psychological Conditions of Personal Engagement and Disengagement at Work," *Academy of Management Journal* 33, no. 4 (1990): 694.

3. Sandra E. Cha and Laura Morgan Roberts, "The Benefits of Bringing Your Whole Identity to Work," *Harvard Business Review* (September 19, 2019): 1–6.

4. James L. Heskett, Thomas O. Jones, Gary W. Loveman, W. Earl Sasser, and Leonard A. Schlesinger, "Putting the Service-Profit Chain to Work," *Harvard Business Review* 72, no. 2 (1994): 164–174.

5. Valerie Bolden-Barrett, "Report: Disengagement Costs Employers up to $500M in Lost Productivity," HR Dive, October 24, 2017, https://www.hrdive.com/news/report-disengagement-costs-employers-up-to-500m-in-lost-productivity/507986/.

6. Edgecumbe Engagement Surveys, available at https://www.edgecumbe.co.uk /engagement-surveys.

7. Address by Anne Francke, CMI Women Conference 2023, May 16, 2023, https://www.youtube.com/watch?v=Yr6Akipln1c&ab_channel=CharteredMan agementInstitute.

8. Tomas Chamorro-Premuzic, "Thriving in the Age of Digital Work," *Harvard Business Review*, January 13, 2021, https://hbr.org/2021/01/thriving-in-the-age -of-hybrid-work.

9. This story may have been invented by President Kennedy as it lacks any confirmation. It fits in the genre of "higher purpose" stories, which are commonplace down through the centuries; however, it was retold in A. M. Carton, "'I'm Not Mopping the Floors, I'm Putting a Man on the Moon': How NASA Leaders Enhanced the Meaningfulness of Work by Changing the Meaning of Work," *Administrative Science Quarterly* 63, no. 2 (2018): 323–369.

10. BBC, "Dunbar's Number: Why We Can Only Maintain 150 Relationships," BBC Future, accessed September 7, 2023, https://www.bbc.com/future/article /20191001-dunbars-number-why-we-can-only-maintain-150-relationships.

11. Jane E. Dutton and Amy Wrzesniewski, "What Job Crafting Looks Like," *Harvard Business Review* (March 12, 2020), https://hbr.org/2020/03/what-job-crafting -looks-like.

12. Ben Laker, Charmi Patel, Pawan Budhwar, and Ashish Malik, "How Job Crafting Can Make Work More Satisfying," *Sloan Management Review* (September 17, 2020), https://sloanreview.mit.edu/article/how-job-crafting-can-make -work-more-satisfying.

Chapter 2

1. Catherine Bailey and Adrian Madden, "What Makes Work Meaningful—Or Meaningless," *MIT Sloan Management Review* (June 1, 2016), https://sloanreview .mit.edu/article/what-makes-work-meaningful-or-meaningless.

2. John D. Eastwood, Alexandra Frischen, Mark J. Fenske, and Daniel Smilek, "The Unengaged Mind: Defining Boredom in Terms of Attention," *Perspectives on Psychological Science* 7, no. 5 (2012): 482–495, http://dx.doi.org/10.1177 /1745691612456044.

3. Lotta Harju, Jari J. Hakanen, and Wilmar B. Schaufeli, "Job Boredom and Its Correlates in 87 Finnish Organizations," *Journal of Occupational and*

Environmental Medicine 56, no. 9 (2014): 911–918, http://dx.doi.org/10.1097
/JOM.0000000000000248; Lia Loukidou, John Loan-Clarke, and Kevin Daniels,
"Boredom in the Workplace: More than Monotonous Tasks," *International Journal of Management Reviews* 11, no. 4 (2009): 381–405, http://dx.doi.org/10.1111
/j.1468-2370.2009.00267.x.

4. Ben Laker, Charmi Patel, Pawan Budhwar, and Ashish Malik, "How Job
Crafting Can Make Work More Satisfying." *MIT Sloan Management Review* (September, 17, 2020), https://sloanreview.mit.edu/article/how-job-crafting-can-make
-work-more-satisfying.

5. Laker, Patel, Budhwar, and Malik, "How Job Crafting Can Make Work More
Satisfying."

6. Bailey and Madden, "What Makes Work Meaningful."

7. Leslie Josephs, "United Airlines Is Sending Employees to Compassion Training," CNBC, March 6, 2018, https://www.cnbc.com/2018/03/06/can-you-teach
-compassion-in-four-hours-united-airlines-is-giving-it-a-go.html.

8. Chloe Lyme, "Is This the Secret to a Perfect Smile? Chinese Flight Attendants
Practise Graceful Grin by Holding a CHOPSTICK between Their Teeth," *Daily
Mail*, January 28, 2016, https://www.dailymail.co.uk/news/peoplesdaily/article
-3420710/Is-secret-perfect-smile-Chinese-flight-attendants-practise-graceful
-grin-holding-CHOPSTICK-teeth.html.

9. Harry McCracken, "How Gmail Happened: The Inside Story of Its Launch 10
Years Ago," *Time*, April 1, 2014, https://time.com/43263/gmail-10th-anniversary.

10. Ryan Tate, "Google Couldn't Kill 20 Percent Time Even if It Wanted To,"
Wired, August 21, 2013, https://www.wired.com/2013/08/20-percent-time-will
-never-die.

11. David Olson, *Managerial Issues of Enterprise Resource Planning Systems* (New
York: McGraw Hill, 2004). The author explores the implications of ERP systems
for the practice of management, using case studies to illustrate the arguments
raised. FoxMeyer's case was particularly significant in this work. For more
examples, visit https://www.computerworld.com/article/2772084/10-famous-erp
-disasters-dustups-and-disappointments.html.

12. Kalle Lyytinen and Rudy Hirschheim, "Information Systems Failures: A
Survey and Classification of the Empirical Literature," *Oxford Surveys in IT* 4,
no. 1 (1987): 257–309. The authors propose the four categories of information
systems failure as highlighted in this chapter.

13. Lebene Soga, Ben Laker, Yemisi Bolade-Ogunfodun, and Marcello Mariani, "Embrace Delegation as a Skill to Strengthen Remote Teams," *MIT Sloan Management Review* 63, no. 1 (2021): 1–3, https://sloanreview.mit.edu/article/embrace-delegation-as-a-skill-to-strengthen-remote-teams. The authors argue a need for delegation to be considered a skill to be honed rather than an activity to be done, thus challenging the traditional views of what delegation entails.

14. Byoungho Ellie Jin, Elena Cedrola, and Naeun (Lauren) Kim, "Process Innovation: Hidden Secret to Success and Efficiency," in *Process Innovation in the Global Fashion Industry*, eds. Byoungho Ellie Jin, and Elena Cedrola (New York: Palgrave Macmillan, 2019), https://doi.org/10.1057/978-1-137-52352-5_1. The authors argue the importance of process innovation as central to operational efficiency in the practice of management. This contrasts with product innovation, which seeks new products for market success.

15. Simon Sinek, *Start with Why: How Great Leaders Inspire Everyone to Take Action* (New York: Penguin, 2011).

16. Amy Wrzesniewski and Jane E. Dutton, "Crafting a Job: Revisioning Employees as Active Crafters of Their Work," *Academy of Management Review* 26, no. 2 (2001): 179–201; Ben Laker, Charmi Patel, Pawan Budhwar, and Ashish Malik, "How Job Crafting Can Make Work More Satisfying," *MIT Sloan Management Review* (September 17, 2020); David Pendleton, Peter Derbyshire, and Chloe Hodgkinson, *Work Life Matters: Crafting a New Balance at Work and at Home* (Cham, Switzerland: Palgrave Macmillan, 2021).

17. Niall Cullinane and Tony Dundon, "The Psychological Contract: A Critical Review," *International Journal of Management Reviews* 8, no. 2 (2006): 113–129, https://doi.org/10.1111/j.1468-2370.2006.00123.x; Denise M. Rousseau, *Psychological Contracts in Organizations: Understanding Written and Unwritten Agreements* (Thousand Oaks, CA: Sage Publications).

18. Josh Lowy, "Overcoming Remote Work Challenges," *MIT Sloan Management Review* (April 9, 2020), https://sloanreview.mit.edu/article/overcoming-remote-work-challenges.

19. Lowy, "Overcoming Remote Work Challenges."

20. Lebene Soga, Bernd Vogel, Ana Margarida Graça, and Kofi Osei-Frimpong, "Web 2.0-Enabled Team Relationships: An Actor-Network Perspective," *European Journal of Work and Organizational Psychology* 30, no. 5 (2020): 639–652, https://doi.org/10.1080/1359432X.2020.1847183. The authors in this work argue how team relationships have become "technologized" as a result of the

active participation of collaborative technologies in teamwork within contemporary organizations.

21. Lebene Soga, Yemisi Bolade-Ogunfodun, and Ben Laker, "Design Your Work Environment to Manage Unintended Tech Consequences," *MIT Sloan Management Review* (September 20, 2021), https://sloanreview.mit.edu/article /design-your-work-environment-to-manage-unintended-tech-consequences/.

22. Soga, Bolade-Ogunfodun, and Laker, "Design Your Work Environment to Manage Unintended Tech Consequences."

23. Ted Coiné and Mark Babbitt, *A World Gone Social: How Companies Must Adapt to Survive* (New York: AMACOM, 2014).

24. Soga, Vogel, Graça, and Osei-Frimpong, "Web 2.0-Enabled Team Relationships."

25. J. C. Rost, "Leadership: A Discussion about Ethics," *Business Ethics Quarterly* 5, no. 1 (1995): 129–142.

Chapter 3

1. Ben Laker, Charmi Patel, Pawan Budhwar, and Ashish Malik, "How Job Crafting Can Make Work More Satisfying," *MIT Sloan Management Review* (September 17, 2020), https://sloanreview.mit.edu/article/how-job-crafting-can-make-work -more-satisfying.

2. Joseph Fuller, Judith K. Wallenstein, Manjari Raman, and Alice de Chalendar, "Your Workforce Is More Adaptable Than You Think," *Harvard Business Review* (May–June, 2019), https://hbr.org/2019/05/your-workforce-is-more-adapta ble-than-you-think.

3. Frank Martela and Derin Kent, "What to Do When Work Feels Meaningless," *Harvard Business Review* (June 3, 2020), https://hbr.org/2020/06/what-to -do-when-work-feels-meaningless.

4. Catherine Bailey and Adrian Madden, "What Makes Work Meaningful—Or Meaningless," *MIT Sloan Management Review* (June 1, 2016), https://sloanreview .mit.edu/article/what-makes-work-meaningful-or-meaningless; Clay Routledge, "You Can't Cure Your Employee's Existential Crisis. But You Can Help," *Harvard Business Review* (June 7, 2021), https://hbr.org/2021/06/you-cant-cure-your -employees-existential-crisis-but-you-can-help?ab=hero-subleft-2.

5. Bailey and Madden, "What Makes Work Meaningful"; Routledge, "You Can't Cure Your Employee's Existential Crisis."

6. Nicholas Bloom, "To Raise Productivity, Let More Employees Work from Home," *Harvard Business Review* (January–February 2014), https://hbr.org/2014 /01/to-raise-productivity-let-more-employees-work-from-home; Lynda Gratton, "Four Principles to Ensure Hybrid Work Is Productive Work," *MIT Sloan Management Review* (November 9, 2020), https://sloanreview.mit.edu/article /four-principles-to-ensure-hybrid-work-is-productive-work.

7. Microsoft, "The Next Great Disruption Is Hybrid Work—Are We Ready?," Work Trend Index Annual Report, March 22, 2021, https://www.microsoft.com /en-us/worklab/work-trend-index/hybrid-work.

8. Rebecca Como, Laura Hambley, and José Domene, "An Exploration of Work-Life Wellness and Remote Work during and beyond COVID-19," *Canadian Journal of Career Development* 20, no. 1 (2020): 46–56.

9. Lucy Kellaway, "The Thin Line between Thick Skin and Complacency," *Financial Times*, June 19, 2012, https://www.ft.com/content/90307af8-eb9e-4ba8 -a085-547ef8b2d61f.

10. Bruno Latour, "Where Are the Missing Masses? A Sociology of a Few Mundane Artifacts," in *Shaping Technology/Building Society: Studies in Sociotechnical Change*, eds. Wiebe Bijker and John Law (pp. 225–258) (Cambridge, MA: MIT Press, 1992).

11. Vision Direct, "How Much Time Do We Spend Looking at Screens?," October 11, 2022, https://www.visiondirect.co.uk/blog/research-reveals-screen-time -habits.

12. James R. Detert and Ethan R. Burris, "Leadership Behavior and Employee Voice: Is the Door Really Open?," *Academy of Management Journal* 50, no. 4 (2007): 869–884, https://doi.org/10.5465/amj.2007.26279183.

13. Wu Liu, Renhong Zhu, Yongkang Yang, "I Warn You Because I Like You: Voice Behavior, Employee Identifications, and Transformational Leadership," *The Leadership Quarterly* 21, no. 1 (2010): 189–202, https://doi.org/10.1016/j .leaqua.2009.10.014.

14. Liping Gao, Onne Janssen, and Kan Shi, "Leader Trust and Employee Voice: The Moderating Role of Empowering Leader Behaviors," *The Leadership Quarterly* 22, no. 4 (2011): 787–798, https://doi.org/10.1016/j.leaqua.2011.05.015.

15. William Bridges, *Jobshift: How to Prosper in a Workplace without Jobs* (Reading, MA: Perseus, 1995).

16. Naina Dhingra, Andrew Samo, Bill Schaninger, and Matt Schrimper, "Help Your Employees Find Purpose or Watch Them Leave," McKinsey, April 5, 2021, https://www.mckinsey.com/business-functions/people-and-organizational-performance/our-insights/help-your-employees-find-purpose-or-watch-them-leave; Bailey and Madden, "What Makes Work Meaningful."

17. Amy Wrzesniewski and Jane E. Dutton, "Crafting a Job: Revisioning Employees as Active Crafters of Their Work," *Academy of Management Review* 26, no. 2 (2001): 179–201.

18. Dhingra, Samo, Schaninger, and Schrimper, "Help Your Employees Find Purpose or Watch Them Leave."

Chapter 4

1. Terrence E. Deal and Allan A. Kennedy, "Culture: A New Look through Old Lenses." *The Journal of Applied Behavioral Science* 19, no. 4 (1983): 498–505.

2. Gerry Johnson, Kevan Scholes, and Richard Whittington, *Exploring Corporate Strategy: Text and Cases* (Harlow, UK: Pearson Education, 2008).

3. Adeyinka Adewale, "A Model of Virtuous Leadership in Africa: Case Study of a Nigerian Firm," *Journal of Business Ethics* 161, no. 4 (2020): 749–762.

4. Sylvi Thun and Arnold B. Bakker, "Empowering Leadership and Job Crafting: The Role of Employee Optimism," *Stress and Health* 34, no. 4 (2018): 573–581.

5. Frederick I. Herzberg, *Work and Nature of Man* (New York: Thomas Y. Crowell, 1966).

6. Ben Laker, Charmi Patel, Pawan Budhwar, and Ashish Malik, "How Job Crafting Can Make Work More Satisfying." *MIT Sloan Management Review* (September, 17, 2020), https://sloanreview.mit.edu/article/how-job-crafting-can-make-work-more-satisfying.

7. Chris Clegg and Caroline Spencer, "A Circular and Dynamic Model of the Process of Job Design," *Journal of Occupational and Organizational Psychology* 80, no. 2 (2007): 321–339.

8. Marilynn B. Brewer and Ya-Ru Chen, "Where (Who) Are Collectives in Collectivism? Toward Conceptual Clarification of Individualism and Collectivism," *Psychological Review* 114, no. 1 (2007): 133.

9. Amy Wrzesniewski and Jane E. Dutton, "Crafting a Job: Revisioning Employees as Active Crafters of Their Work," *Academy of Management Review* 26, no. 2 (2001): 179–201.

10. Mihaly Csikszentmihalyi, *Creativity: Flow and the Psychology of Discovery and Invention* (New York: HarperPerennial, 1997).

11. For example, see Jari J. Hakanen, Piia Seppälä, and Maria C. W. Peeters, "High Job Demands, Still Engaged and Not Burned Out? The Role of Job Crafting," *International Journal of Behavioral Medicine* 24 (2017): 619–627; Lotta K. Harju, Janne Kaltiainen, and Jari J. Hakanen, "The Double-Edged Sword of Job Crafting: The Effects of Job Crafting on Changes in Job Demands and Employee Well-Being," *Human Resource Management* 60, no. 6 (2021): 953–968; Hiroyuki Toyama, Katja Upadyaya, and Katariina Salmela-Aro, "Job Crafting and Well-Being among School Principals: The Role of Basic Psychological Need Satisfaction and Frustration," *European Management Journal* 40, no. 5 (2022): 809–818.

Chapter 5

1. E. Thomas Moran and J. Fredericks Volkwein, "The Cultural Approach to the Formation of Organisational Climate," *Human Relations* 45, no. 1 (1992): 19–47. Definition is on page 20.

2. Edgar H. Schein, "Defining Organizational Culture," *Classics of Organization Theory* 3, no. 1 (1985): 490–502.

3. Moran and Volkwein, "The Cultural Approach to the Formation of Organisational Climate."

4. Black Ashforth, "Climate Formation: Issues and Extensions," *Academy of Management Review* 10, no. 4 (1985): 837–847.

5. Peter Kangis, D. Gordon, and S. Williams, "Organisational Climate and Corporate Performance: An Empirical Investigation," *Management Decision* 38, no. 8 (2000): 531–540.

6. Amy Lyman, "Building Trust in the Workplace," *Strategic HR Review* 3, no. 1 (2003): 24–27.

Chapter 6

1. Daniel H. Pink, *Drive: The Surprising Truth about What Motivates Us* (New York: Penguin, 2011).

2. "Activity Based Working in Action: WeWork, Costa Coffee and Gerson Lehrman Group," Midwich, November 14, 2022, https://www.midwich.com /news-and-events/blogs/activity-based-working-in-action-wework-costa-coffee -and-glg.

3. Armin Falk and Michael Kosfeld, "The Hidden Costs of Control," *American Economic Review* 96, no. 5 (2006): 1611–1630.

4. Edward L. Deci and Richard M. Ryan, "The 'What' and 'Why' of Goal Pursuits: Human Needs and the Self Determination of Behavior," *Psychological Inquiry* 11, no. 4 (2000): 227–268.

5. Edward L. Deci and Richard M. Ryan, "Self-Determination Theory." *International Encyclopedia of the Social & Behavioral Sciences* 2 (2015): 486–491, https:// doi.org/10.1016/b978-0-08-097086-8.26036-4.

6. Janet Polivy and C. Peter Herman, "If at First You Don't Succeed: False Hopes of Self-Change," *American Psychologist* 57, no. 9 (2002): 677.

7. M. W. Gallagher, "Self-Efficacy." *Encyclopedia of Human Behavior* (2012) 314–320, https://doi.org/10.1016/b978-0-12-375000-6.00312-8.

8. John Stuart Mill, *Principles of Political Economy* (Oxford: Oxford University Press, 1994 [1848]).

9. Adeyinka Adewale, "Cross-Functional Teams" Workshop 1, Organisations and People, Henley Business School, Henley-on-Thames, October 23, 2021.

10. J. Richard Hackman and Greg R. Oldham. "The Job Diagnostic Survey: An Instrument for the Diagnosis of Jobs and the Evaluation of Job Redesign Projects," technical report, Dept. of Administrative Sciences, Yale University, New Haven, CT, May 1974.

11. Peter B. Warr, "Decision Latitude, Job Demands, and Employee Well-Being," *Work & Stress* 4, no. 4 (1990): 285–294.

12. Giedrius Vanagas and Susanna Bihari-Axelsson, "Interaction among General Practitioners Age and Patient Load in the Prediction of Job Strain, Decision Latitude and Perception of Job Demands: A Cross-Sectional Study," *BMC Public Health* 4 (2004): 1–6.

13. Ben Laker, Charmi Patel, Pawan Budhwar, and Ashish Malik, "How Job Crafting Can Make Work More Satisfying." *MIT Sloan Management Review* (September, 17, 2020), https://sloanreview.mit.edu/article/how-job-crafting-can-make -work-more-satisfying.

14. Nathaniel Koloc, "Let Employees Choose When, Where, and How to Work," *Harvard Business Review* (November 22, 2014), https://hbr.org/2014/11/let-employees-choose-when-where-and-how-to-work.

15. Chamu Sundaramurthy, "Sustaining Trust within Family Businesses," *Family Business Review* 21, no. 1 (2008): 89–102.

16. Brianna Provenzano, "The Takeaway: Inclusive Leadership: How We Lead Online and Offline," NationSwell, January 20, 2023, https://nationswell.com/the-takeaway-inclusive-leadership-how-we-lead-online-and-offline.

17. Stephen Bungay, *The Art of Action: How Leaders Close the Gap between Plans, Actions, and Results* (London: Nicholas Brealey, 2022).

18. Janet Choi, "Cells, Pods, and Squads: The Future of Organizations Is Small" (blog), revised 2019 [2014], http://blog.idonethis.com/cells-pods-squads-structure.

19. "Oil and Gas Skills Strategy Reveals Rapidly Changing Sector," OPITO, May 2, 2019, https://opito.com/media/news/oil-and-gas-skills-strategy-reveals-rapidly-changing-sector.

20. "Majority of UK Offshore Workforce to Be Delivering Low Carbon Energy by 2030," Robert Gordon University, May 26, 2021, https://www.rgu.ac.uk/news/news-2021/4157-majority-of-uk-offshore-workforce-to-be-delivering-low-carbon-energy-by-2030.

21. Kirsty Denyer and Tatiana S. Rowson. 2022. "'I've Finally Got My Expression': The Anchoring Role of Identity in Changing from an Organisation-Based Career to a Protean Career Path," *British Journal of Guidance & Counselling* (April 2022): 1–11, https://doi.org/10.1080/03069885.2022.2045570.

22. Selin Kudret, Berrin Erdogan, and Talya N. Bauer, "Self-Monitoring Personality Trait at Work: An Integrative Narrative Review and Future Research Directions," *Journal of Organizational Behavior* 40, no. 2 (2019): 193–208.

23. Chartered Institute of Personnel and Development, "UK Working Lives: The CIPD Job Quality Index," 2019, https://www.cipd.org/globalassets/media/zzz-misc---to-check/uk-working-lives-2019-v1_tcm18-58585.pdf.

24. Alastair Cameron, "Coronavirus and Homeworking in the UK: April 2020," Office of National Statistics, July 8, 2020, https://www.ons.gov.uk/employmentandlabourmarket/peopleinwork/employmentandemployeetypes/bulletins/coronavirusandhomeworkingintheuk/april2020.

25. Erich C. Dierdorff and Jaclyn M. Jensen, "Crafting in Context: Exploring When Job Crafting Is Dysfunctional for Performance Effectiveness," *Journal of Applied Psychology* 103, no. 5 (2018): 463–477.

26. Gregory A. Laurence, Yitzhak Fried, Wan Yan, and Jie Li, "Enjoyment of Work and Driven to Work as Motivations of Job Crafting: Evidence from Japan and China," *Japanese Psychological Research* 62, no. 1 (2020): 1–13.

27. Lonneke Dubbelt, Evangelia Demerouti, and Sonja Rispens, "The Value of Job Crafting for Work Engagement, Task Performance, and Career Satisfaction: Longitudinal and Quasi-Experimental Evidence," *European Journal of Work & Organizational Psychology* 28, no. 3 (2019): 300–314.

28. Ryan D. Duffy, Bryan J. Dik, and Michael F. Steger, "Calling and Work-Related Outcomes: Career Commitment as a Mediator," *Journal of Vocational Behavior* 78, no. 2 (2011): 210–218.

Chapter 7

1. Arnold B. Bakker and Evangelia Demerouti, "The Job Demands-Resources Model: State of the Art," *Journal of Managerial Psychology* 22, no. 3 (2007): 209–328, at 312.

2. Patricia Baratta and Jeffrey R. Spence, "Do Bored Employees Job Craft When Demands and Resources Are Low?," in *Academy of Management Proceedings 2017*, ed. Sonia Taneja (Briarcliff Manor, NY: Academy of Management), 14363.

3. Arnold B. Bakker, Evangelia Demerouti, and Ana Isabel Sanz-Vergel, "Burnout and Work Engagement: The JD–R Approach," *The Annual Review of Organizational Psychology and Organizational Behavior* 1, no. 1 (2014): 389–411.

4. Teresa M. Amabile, *Creativity in Context* (Boulder, CO: Westview Press, 1996).

5. Michael D. Mumford, Ginamarie M. Scott, Blaine Gaddis, and Jill M. Strange, "Leading Creative People: Orchestrating Expertise and Relationships," *Leadership Quarterly* 13, no. 6 (2002): 705–750.

6. Christina E. Shalley and Greg R. Oldham, "Competition and Creative Performance: Effects of Competitor Presence and Visibility," *Creativity Research Journal* 10, no. 4 (1997): 337–345.

7. Markus Baer, Greg R. Oldham, and Anne Cummings, "Rewarding Creativity: When Does It Really Matter?," *The Leadership Quarterly* 14, nos. 4–5 (2003): 569–586.

8. Baer, Oldham, and Cummings, "Rewarding Creativity."

9. Jos Akkermans, Veerle Brenninkmeijer, Marthe Huibers, and Roland W. B. Blonk, "Competencies for the Contemporary Career: Development and Preliminary Validation of the Career Competencies Questionnaire," *Journal of Career Development* 40, no. 3 (2013): 245–267.

10. Maria Tims, Arnold B. Bakker, and Daantje Derks, "The Impact of Job Crafting on Job Demands, Job Resources, and Well-being," *Journal of Occupational Health Psychology* 18, no. 2 (2013): 230–240.

Chapter 8

1. Jeffrey Hayzlett, "Is the Gig Economy Killing the 9-to-5 Job? No, but It's Giving It a Run for Its Money," Entrepreneur, March 16, 2018, https://www .entrepreneur.com/business-news/is-the-gig-economy-killing-the-9-to-5-job-no -but-its/310368.

2. A. M. Carton, "'I'm Not Mopping the Floors, I'm Putting a Man on the Moon': How NASA Leaders Enhanced the Meaningfulness of Work by Changing the Meaning of Work," *Administrative Science Quarterly* 63, no. 2 (2018): 323–369.

Index

Tools for job crafting (cont.)
  case study, 94–96
  decision latitude, 86–92
  hiring and, 92–93
Training and development, 12–13,
    22, 59, 69, 76–77, 108–110, 123
Transparency, 31–32, 93–94, 115
Trust, 25, 31, 88–89
Trusting the process, 38–39, 43, 55,
    73–75

UK National Health Service, 19, 109
United Airlines, 22
United Kingdom oil and gas sector,
    94–96
University of Michigan, 106
Upworthy, 89
US Internal Revenue Service, 24

Values
  conflict of, 20–21
  defined, 56
  organizational, 53–58, 63
  permission to craft and, 60–64
  personal, 60–61, 63–64, 117
  relational crafting and, 29–30
Vision Direct, 42

Well-being, 13, 55, 69, 83–84, 97, 99,
    102, 106, 108, 111. *See also* Mental
    and physical health
Wilson, Timothy D., 4
WordPress, 93
Work from home. *See* Flexible
    working arrangements
Workloads, 87–88, 101–103, 122
Workshops, 106, 123
Wrzesniewski, Amy, 45